The Healing Spirit

The Healing Spirit

A STUDY OF SEVEN JOURNEYS TO RECOVERY
FROM CHILDHOOD SEXUAL ABUSE

LEO O. STOSSICH

Foreword by Stuart C. Devenish

WIPF *&* STOCK · Eugene, Oregon

THE HEALING SPIRIT
A Study of Seven Journeys to Recovery from Childhood Sexual Abuse

Copyright © 2019 Leo O. Stossich. All rights reserved. Except for brief quotations in critical publications or reviews, no part of this book may be reproduced in any manner without prior written permission from the publisher. Write: Permissions, Wipf and Stock Publishers, 199 W. 8th Ave., Suite 3, Eugene, OR 97401.

Wipf & Stock
An Imprint of Wipf and Stock Publishers
199 W. 8th Ave., Suite 3
Eugene, OR 97401

www.wipfandstock.com

PAPERBACK ISBN: 978-1-5326-4427-6
HARDCOVER ISBN: 978-1-5326-4428-3
EBOOK ISBN: 978-1-5326-4429-0

Manufactured in the U.S.A.   01/03/19

All Scripture quotations unless otherwise indicated, are taken from the Holy Bible, New Revised Standard Version, NRSV. Copyright © 1989 the Division of Christian Education of the National Council of the Churches of Christ in the United States of America. Used by permission. All rights reserved.

I dedicate this book to the many victims of childhood sexual abuse who are yet to tell their story; who are yet to be really listened to; and who are yet to find their pathway to healing. I pray you encounter the love of Christ through his church on your journey.

CONTENTS

List of Tables | *xi*
Foreword by Stuart C. Devenish | *xiii*
Preface | *xvii*
Acknowledgments | *xix*
Abbreviations | *xx*
Introduction | *xxi*

1. **Childhood Sexual Abuse and Christian Ministry** | 1
   Defining the Problem | 1
   The Prevalence, Impact, and Nature of the Problem | 2
   The Spiritual Dimension of the Problem | 5
   The Church and Christian Ministry | 9
   Conclusion | 12

2. **A Biblical/Theological Exploration of Spiritual Ministry** | 13
   Introduction | 13
   Metaphors, Models, and Theologies of Salvation in the New Testament | 13
   Salvation and Healing | 19
   The Church and Ministry | 25
   Conclusion | 29

3. **Biographical and Healing Narratives** | 31
   Introducing the Participants | 32
   The Interpretative Themes | 37
   Conclusion | 38

4. **The World as the Context For the Activity of the Holy Spirit** | 39
   Introduction | 39
   Dysfunctionality and Damage | 40
   Deprivation and Disempowerment | 41

Disillusionment with Religion | 41
Conversion and Change | 42
Christian Heritage | 43
Discovering God | 43
Relationship with God | 44
Faith and Calling | 44
Summary | 45
The Lived World of Perceptual Phenomena | 45
The Self and the Other in Relation | 48
Transcendence and Immanence | 51
Conclusion | 54

5. Woundedness | 55

Introduction | 55
Vulnerability, Manipulation, and Control | 55
Internal Damage | 56
Inner and Outer Worlds | 57
Images of God | 58
Uncovering Wounds | 58
Rising Emotions | 59
Oversexualization | 60
Summary | 60
Self as Myth-Maker | 61
Self and World Discovered in Experience | 66
Human Beings as Existentially Vulnerable | 68
Conclusion | 72

6. Faith Community | 73

Introduction | 73
Spiritual Foundations | 73
Encouraging Influences | 74
Personal and Spiritual Growth | 75
Cultivating the Spiritual Life | 75
Community and Identity | 76
Mixed Church Experiences | 76
Counseling and Prayer | 77
Ministerial Life and Experience | 77
Summary | 78
Communion with God Involving Community with Others | 78
Community as Spiritual and Personal Formation | 81

    Christian Community as Openness to God's Promised Future | 85
    Conclusion | 88

7. Healing | 90
    Introduction | 90
    Remembering and Understanding | 90
    Naming Abuse | 91
    Disclosing Abuse | 91
    Depth and Need | 92
    Facilitators to Healing | 92
    Inhibitors and Relapses | 93
    Trust and Safety | 93
    Forgiveness and Healing | 94
    Identity and Purpose | 95
    Healing and Wholeness | 96
    Summary | 96
    Human Knowing as Transformative | 97
    Human Love as Supportive of Deeper Knowing | 102
    Intimacy in God's Love as Healing | 108
    Conclusion | 112

8. The Holy Spirit | 114
    Introduction | 114
    The Flame of the Spirit | 114
    Interventions and Interruptions | 115
    Revelation and Change | 115
    Event and Process | 116
    Infilling of the Holy Spirit | 116
    Guidance and Counseling | 117
    Overwhelming Help from the Spirit | 118
    The Spirit and Christ | 118
    Summary | 119
    The Actualizing of New Life Capacities as the Spirit | 119
    The Impetus, Confidence, and Courage for Change as the Spirit | 125
    The Movement Toward Shared Life as the Spirit | 133
    Conclusion | 139

9. A Model for Spiritual Ministry to Victims of Childhood Sexual Abuse | 141
    Introduction | 141
    The Work of the Spirit in Healing | 141

 The Work of the Spirit and Ministerial Practice | 144
 Implications for Pastoral Education | 149
 Concluding Statement | 150

Appendix 1 | 153

Appendix 2 | 155

Appendix 3 | 156

Bibliography | 159

LIST OF TABLES

3.1 The forty-one interpretative themes identified have been assigned under the headings for chapters 4–8.

FOREWORD

Stuart C. Devenish

I REMEMBER IT LIKE it was yesterday. I was a pastor in the middle years of my ministry. I accompanied a young man who had recently joined my faith community to a neighboring church where he would make two uncomfortable accusations. The first was that the ministry leader in that church had abused him sexually as a child. And the second was that his denomination had actively tried to cover up the abuse. It was a nasty, dirty business. There were no winners—least of all the young man I was seeking to support. Now, the findings of the 2017 Australian Royal Commission in Institutional Responses to Child Sex Abuse are reverberating around the corridors of Australian institutions (including the Churches). Following the visit to Ireland by Pope Francis in August 2018, where he apologized for extensive clergy sexual abuse in that country, he declared, "We showed no care for the little ones." No one can doubt that childhood sexual abuse is a problem of mega-proportions.

Many people think the blame for sexual abuse can be laid at the door of the churches like some abandoned child. The logic goes: the church is the dispenser of goodness and grace, but when its own people act in unholy and unseemly ways, they disprove their own creed. There is truth in this, of course, but the accusation is only partly right because the sexual revolution that has unfolded in Western society since the late 1960s has affected everyone, not just the Church. Everyone must deal with the fallout from the sexual revolution that continues to play out in every sector of society. It is impossible to answer the question who won in the moral battlefield that was the culture wars. The only option is to support those who lost the most. I think there are three clear losers. The first is morality and goodness itself. The institution of family, moral people, and all processes of healthy, personal formation have paid a heavy price.

The second are children who—without the power to defend themselves—can find themselves caught in webs of adult sexual predation that are harmful and destructive. As the author of this book states, when deep trust is betrayed by significant others in children's lives, a kind of "soul destruction" occurs. Recovering from such fracking in their personal lives represents a profound challenge to children who are still in formation. The third are young people growing up at a time when pornography has become normalized, same-sex relationships are on the agenda, and casual sex via "hook-ups" on social media are seen as recreation. Where is there any space for personal wholeness and virtue ethics to flourish and for properly functioning people to be formed?

This book takes us to some hard places. It forces us to address deep questions at the core of our humanity. Once a sexual or moral offense has been committed against a child, is it possible to find healing and recover any kind of proper intimacy? Or are victims of childhood sexual abuse destined to be fractured people living in broken institutions existing in a shattered world for the remainder of their lives?

This author insists that a whole person healing *is* available to men and women, boys and girls, victims and perpetrators, parents and families, churches and communities. It is the kind of transformative healing that C. S. Lewis spoke of when he referred to God's "deep magic." It *can* be utterly transformative, totally life-changing, and has the capacity to rebuild broken trust, shattered dreams, and ruined innocence. According to the real-world research provided in this book, that kind of healing comes from the Spirit of Christ who is at work in the lives of every human being on the planet, and who whispers hope to every soul, befriending, healing and loving from the inside, in the place of their deepest hopes and fears.

The American episcopal Bishop Currie, in his address at the Royal wedding of Prince Harry and Megan Markle, spoke of the reality of the love of God that overwhelms and underpins our lives as people from the inside out. Siegel is quoted in this text as saying, "The truth is, only love heals." Although not everyone is capable of seeing it, Christianity is the "only place where God provides all that is needed to heal and make whole a lost humanity."

The seven case studies offered by the author have arisen out of in-depth research based on actual people. These case studies make for painful, engaging, fascinating, and hopeful reading. I have watched this research come to birth over the years from first concept to research thesis to published book. The methodology that underpins this research is phenomenology. It is strong and trustworthy. The simplest definition of phenomenology is as a stethoscope to the soul that can explain the impulses of the human heart. It gives us a view of what is happening inside of persons, including ourselves. That makes it a particularly acute tool for this kind of inner-life research.

This text has something important to say to everyone who comes to it with an open mind. Whether the reader is a victim, family member, member of the general public (with or without faith), pastoral care practitioner, counsellor or psychologist . . . there are words of wisdom addressed to each of us. The challenge for readers of this text is to become their brother's and sister's keeper and protector. A good society is the one where boys and girls can grow up to achieve their full potential, intellectually, vocationally, creatively, personally, morally, spiritually, and sexually.

The Christian gospel is an invitation to wholeness, to rightness, to fullness, and to wellness. It is an utter tragedy when anyone or anything blocks a child's path to their God-given potential. And when life delivers us a deck of cards over which we have no control, such as trauma, wounding, and childhood sexual abuse, it too is a tragedy of unspeakable proportions if there is no way back to healing and wholeness. Thank God there is a journey of healing, recovery, and of hopeful restoration available. No, it is not a simple mail-order transaction. But it is real, and it is possible.

There is a scene in Tolkien's *Lord of the Rings* movie where Gandalf, Legolas, Gimli, and Aragorn are confronted by the Army of the Dead on the Dimholt Road whose leader speaks the words, "The way is shut. It was made by those who are dead." The writer of this book says something very different. He says the way to recovery and healing is open. And it is available to those who ask, seek, and knock. The invitation is to all who seek life to enter and be healed.

>Stuart C. Devenish
>Director of Postgraduate Studies
>Tabor College of Higher Education,
>Adelaide, South Australia.
>Stuart is a specialist in the field of Christian spirituality

PREFACE

THE IMPETUS FOR MY doctoral thesis, on which this book is based, grew out of several personal convictions that have developed over more than thirty-five years of pastoral practice. The first is one every Christian leader would fully endorse; namely, making disciples is a mandatory ministry of every local church. Jesus made this imperative before his ascension. The second conviction, which may not be as obvious, is that in order for this to occur, we must provide opportunity for young disciples to grow and mature, and we must provide opportunity for wounded disciples to find healing from past traumas. The church cannot truly disciple all people if it is not a healing community. The third conviction is that healing occurs in an environment where survivors can be attentive to the voice of the Holy Spirit, who is the love of God poured into human hearts. It is the love of God that heals, frees, and empowers growth toward wholeness and maturity in people. These three points have led me to a fourth conviction. I believe that the human experience of the Holy Spirit's work in the depth of woundedness to bring about restoration and healing should inform every aspect and area of Christian ministry, that is, our preaching, teaching, helping, praying, and communicating with one another.

I would like to express my deep appreciation to the seven persons who volunteered to participate in my doctoral research project which investigated healing for Christian believers from the devastation of childhood sexual abuse. I applaud each of them for their courage in being so willingly open, honest, and vulnerable. Each of them are teachers for the church and the world at large, though often silent. I am privileged to be able to echo and amplify their voices. I trust that their journeys will inspire and enable us to more fully integrate the work of the Holy Spirit in all we do.

Leo O. Stossich

ACKNOWLEDGMENTS

I WISH TO THANK each participant in my research project. I also wish to thank my wife Rosemary for her continual encouragement and support for me in completing this book.

ABBREVIATIONS

Gen	Genesis
Num	Numbers
Ps	Psalms
Isa	Isaiah
Joel	Joel
Matt	The Gospel According to Matthew
Mark	The Gospel According to Mark
Luke	The Gospel According to Luke
Acts	The Acts of the Apostles
Rom	The Epistle to the Romans
1 Cor	The First Epistle to the Corinthians
2 Cor	The Second Epistle to the Corinthians
Gal	The Epistle to the Galatians
Eph	The Epistle to the Ephesians
Phil	The Epistle to the Philippians
Heb	The Epistle to the Hebrews
NASB	New American Standard Bible

INTRODUCTION

CHILDHOOD SEXUAL ABUSE REPRESENTS a fundamental problem for Western society. Its malicious effects can be found in populations across our cities, suburbs, towns, and farms. Clinical and pastoral experience, as well as ongoing research, suggests victims of childhood sexual abuse suffer lifelong harm or devastation as a result of abuse perpetrated by trusted others. The Royal Commission into Child Sexual Abuse in Australian Institutions represents a direct response to this problem. Religious institutions are featured in those enquiries because a proportion of the abuse has been perpetrated on the innocent by church members and leaders themselves.

Furthermore, a persistent factor in pastoral ministry is the presence of women and men in our churches who have been sexually abused as children but have remained unrecognized, unhelped, and unhealed. Some of these victims are involved in the activities and ministries of the church and adjust to their pain through self-deception or mask their suffering with smiles and overinvolvement. If one understands the Church to be a conglomerate of mini faith communities where openness, safety, intimacy, healing, and growth are to be the norm, then one may well be puzzled, disappointed, or even angry by reports of adult victims of childhood sexual abuse who have come to faith in Christ, but continue to suffer in silence—either for extended periods of time or even throughout their lifetime, rather than disclosing their turmoil and finding help through ministry in their faith community.

The Christian ideal is to release victims from their woundedness and oppression and restore them to the wellbeing and wholeness available in the Kingdom of God. But as a whole, the Christian community has been slow to grasp the severity and extent of the problem or to provide the healing resources of the Gospel in keeping with the teachings of Jesus Christ.

Nonetheless, some victims claim to have experienced recovery through the various ministries of local churches and the transformative

Introduction

power of Christian spirituality. These victims claim to have been enabled to move beyond their pain and debilitation to a place of restored wellbeing. While the sordid memories linger, the pain and suffering are removed, and the recovered victims are able to live in the present as restored people who can sustain appropriate levels of psychological stability, appropriate sexual intimacy with their spouses, and a growing level of spiritual maturity.

This book is based on research I undertook into the healing journeys of seven recovered victims. The research involved undertaking in-depth interviews to elicit and phenomenologically explore the autobiographical narratives of seven victims' accounts of their spiritual healing journeys. The internal desecration[1] sustained by these persons and their ensuing healing journey renders their narratives invaluable in terms of exploring the most original and important source of information on the activity of the Holy Spirit in healing.

It involved attending to the victims' experiences of abuse, including their earliest memories; the nature, severity, and duration of the abuse; their changing understandings of the abuse experiences; and the short- and long-term impacts that resulted from the emotional, psychological, and spiritual abuse. It also involved attending to their spiritual journey including their backgrounds and upbringing, their involvement with churches and Christians, and those events and persons that have been significant for them. It also involved attending to their healing journeys, including their many attempts at recovery, the ministry of the church in facilitating recovery, and the changes that led to healing.

The recovered victims attributed their healing transformations to the activity of the Holy Spirit encountered in the context of the pastoral ministry of the local church. While the Spirit is an entity hidden to us in healing, I wanted to explore the experiences of recovered victims from which meaning for the work of the Spirit in healing and Christian ministry can be disclosed.

In chapter 1, we will focus on childhood sexual abuse as a spiritual problem requiring spiritual restoration and seek to understand this in relation to the spiritual ministry of the local church. In chapter 2, an understanding will be developed of the activity of the Holy Spirit in spiritual healing from both the New Testament and theological literature. In chapter

---

1. The term *internal desecration* is taken from Doehring's research entitled *Internal Desecration: Traumatization and Representations of God* and is briefly explained in chapter 1.

Introduction

3, we will survey the biographical and healing narratives of the recovered victims derived from interviews, in order to explore meaning for the activity of the Holy Spirit in relation to their experiences of recovery.

The following five chapters come to the heart of the matter by exploring the experiences of the recovered victims to discover meaning for the human experience of the activity of the Holy Spirit in relation to their recovery.

The final chapter, chapter 9, will discuss those core themes which have emerged from the recovered victims' experiences of the activity of the Holy Spirit in healing from the devastation of childhood sexual abuse within the context of the life and ministry of the local church.

1

CHILDHOOD SEXUAL ABUSE AND CHRISTIAN MINISTRY

Defining the Problem

PROVIDING A PROPER DEFINITION to the term "sexual abuse" is complicated by the varied relationships that exist between victims and perpetrators. For example, sexual behavior between two adolescents may or may not be considered abusive, depending upon whether the behavior was consensual, whether there was coercion, or whether there was equality in the relationship.[1] In Australia, consensual sexual activity between a twenty-year-old and a fifteen-year-old is considered abusive, while the same activity between a twenty-year-old and a seventeen-year-old is not. In instances of intra-familial sexual abuse, the concepts of consent, equality, and coercion are inapplicable. The behaviors described by the seven recovered victims in this book would be considered to be sexually abusive by almost everyone.

Tomison defines childhood sexual abuse as "the use of a child for sexual gratification by an adult or significantly older child/adolescent."[2] Broadbent and Bentley define it as "any act which exposes a child to, or involves a child in, sexual processes beyond his or her understanding or contrary to acceptable community standards."[3] These general definitions of

---

1. Ryan, "Sexually Abusive Youth," 3–9.
2. Tomison, "Update on Childhood Sexual Abuse," 2.
3. Broadbent and Bentley, "Child Abuse and Neglect," 14.

childhood sexual abuse are apt descriptions of the early sexual experiences of the seven recovered victims in this book.

Children always have less power than adults, and so the sexual abuse of a child occurs when a person uses their authority, either by using force or not, to get a child to participate in activities that are for the adult's or older person's sexual gratification. The closer the relationship between the child and the adult here, the greater the dependency and the greater the power that the adult has over the child.

The Australian Institute of Family Studies succinctly defines the problem:

> Sexually abusive behavior refers to any sexual activity between an adult and a child below the age of consent; non-consensual sexual activity between minors (e.g., a fourteen-year-old and a ten-year-old); or any sexual activity between a child under eighteen years old and a person in a position of power or authority (e.g., parent, teacher). Sexual activity includes fondling genitals, masturbation, oral sex, vaginal or anal penetration by a penis, finger or any other object, fondling of breast, voyeurism, exhibitionism and exposing or involving the child in pornography.[4]

The Prevalence, Impact, and Nature of the Problem

Research has provided some indication of the prevalence, impact, and nature of the problem of childhood sexual abuse. The sexual abuse of children is widely regarded to occur at significant levels in the Australian community and to be a cause of mental health issues in adult life. An indication of the prevalence of the problem has been provided by numerous studies.[5] The April 2010 resource sheet of The Australian Institute of Family Studies estimated the child sexual abuse range to be one-in-two to one-in-four for girls, and one-in-four to one-in-six for boys.[6] The Australian Institute of Family Studies indicates that,

> Studies that comprehensively measured the prevalence of child sexual abuse found that males had prevalence rates of four to eight per cent for penetrative abuse and twelve to sixteen per cent

---

4. Price-Robertson et al., "Prevalence of Child Abuse," 5.

5. Finkelhor, *Child Sexual Abuse*; Herman et al., *Long-term Effects of Incestuous Abuse in Childhood*; Kinsey et al., *Sexual Behavior in the Human Female*; Meiselman, *Incest*.

6. Price-Robertson et al., "The Prevalence of Child Abuse and Neglect."

for non-penetrative abuse, while females had prevalence rates of seven to twelve per cent for penetrative abuse and twenty-three to thirty-six per cent for non-penetrative abuse.[7]

It is further understood that many cases of the sexual abuse of children remain hidden.

A global meta-analysis published in 2014 estimated that prevalence rates of childhood sexual abuse in Australia are 22 percent for females and 8 percent for males. The study also indicated that Australia has the highest prevalence rate for girls worldwide.[8]

Childhood sexual abuse is a multi-dimensional problem which impacts the individual, the family, and the community in serious and disturbing ways both in its initial effects and long-term consequences.[9] There may be initial negative symptoms in children, and further problems which develop, intrude, and persist throughout a survivor's lifetime.[10] A review of forty-five studies demonstrated that sexually abused children clearly displayed more problem-symptoms than did non-abused children.[11] While no one symptom is characteristic of a majority of sexually abused children, the literature widely indicates that the initial effects of childhood sexual abuse may include: medical problems such as sexually transmitted diseases; pregnancy and physical injury; emotional problems such as guilt, anger, hostility, anxiety, fear, post-traumatic stress disorder, shame, and lowered self-esteem; behavioral problems such as aggression, delinquency, sexualized behavior, nightmares, phobias, eating and sleeping disorders; and, school problems and truancy. The full impact may be only gradually realized over many years as the abused child emerges as a dysfunctional adult.

The long-term consequences are still being documented, but there are strong indications that experiences of sexual abuse as a child may lead to negative physical, cognitive, psychological, or social consequences in

---

7. Price-Robertson et al., "Prevalence of Child Abuse," 5.

8. Stoltenborgh et al., "A Global Perspective."

9. The early reactions are often called *short-term* effects in the literature. Brown and Finkelhor prefer *initial* effects because "short-term" implies that the reactions do not persist—an assumption that has not been substantiated.

10. Briere and Runtz, "Suicidal Thoughts and Behaviours," 413–23; Conte and Schuerman, "Factors Associated," 201–11; Courtois, "Healing the Incest Wound," 464–97; Salter, "Epidemiology of Child Sexual Abuse." 108–38; Summit, "Child Sexual Abuse Accommodation Syndrome," 177–93; Terr, "Childhood Traumas," 10–20; Van der Kolk et al., *Traumatic Stress*.

11. Kendall-Tackett et al., "Impact of Sexual Abuse," 164–80.

adulthood.[12] These may include: sexual dysfunction (such as flashbacks, difficulty in arousal, avoidance of, or phobic reactions to, sexual intimacy); promiscuity; prostitution; discomfort in intimate relationships; isolation; marital problems; low self-esteem; depression; mental health problems; drug or alcohol abuse; eating disorders; and suicide. The kinds of child sexual abuse that seem to be the most damaging are experiences involving father figures, genital contact, and force.[13] Mullen and Fleming surmise that the fundamental damage inflicted by child sexual abuse is to the child's developing capacities for trust, intimacy, agency, and sexuality and that many of the mental health problems of adult life may be second-order effects.[14]

It is well established within the field of trauma research that childhood sexual abuse affects a child's developing sense of self.[15] It is during childhood that the foundation of identity is laid.[16] A meta-analysis of the published research on the effects of childhood sexual abuse provided clear evidence of the link between the abuse and subsequent negative and long-term effects on development.[17] The psychological structures of the self and basic assumptions about oneself, in terms of self-definition, self-perception, and the world, are significantly affected.[18] As such, the human-induced trauma associated with childhood sexual abuse is "a special category of trauma."[19] It carries *a unique devastation factor* as it distorts foundational realities of what it means to be human as,

> . . . embodied personhood is plundered, delegated authority becomes destructive, sexual expression is perverted, intrapersonal trust is shattered, and profound metaphors for God are disfigured.[20]

Childhood sexual abuse misshapes the early self, which is always a social self, stripping its orientation of being from being-in-relation. It becomes a victim of crushing alienation desperately needing affirmation it

12. Lamont, "Effects of Child Abuse."
13. Browne and Finkelhor, "Impact of Child Sexual Abuse," 66–77.
14. Mullen and Fleming, *Long-term Effects.*.
15. Crowley, *The Search for Autonomous Intimacy*; Herman, *Trauma and Recovery*; Roche et al., "Adult Attachment," 184–207.
16. Josselson, *Finding Herself*; Josselson, *Revising Herself.*
17. Paolucci et al., "A Meta-Analysis," 17–37.
18. Phillips and Daniluk, "Beyond 'Survivor,'" 177–84.
19. Means, *Trauma & Evil*, 1.
20. Schmutzer, "A Theology of Sexual Abuse," 785–812.

can no longer risk.[21] If *evil* is understood as "a process that divides persons within and against themselves and separates them from their necessary relationships with the world, others, and God," then human-induced trauma, of this kind, is "an expression of evil."[22] The devastation of personality structures resulting from sexual abuse as a child has been likened to *soul murder*.[23] Doehring uses temple imagery to describe childhood sexual abuse as "a desecration of the inner sanctum" and "the smashing of internal representations of God."[24] Herman says that "to study psychological trauma [of this kind] is to come face-to-face . . . with the capacity for evil in human nature."[25] Van der Kolk and McFarlane state the following:

> There are aspects of the experience of trauma that cannot be captured in medical and scientific models, but that go to the core of what it is like to be human . . . [as] scientific, empirical frameworks . . . leave little room for the vital human dimensions affected by trauma: Attitudes toward trauma and victimization must . . . reflect people's basic beliefs about what it means to be human, and people's positions about the eternal questions of good and evil.[26]

While working with trauma is clearly in the purview of science (e.g., psychology and physiology), addressing problems of evil involves the moral, ethical, and spiritual dimensions of life.

The Spiritual Dimension of the Problem

Within the last few decades, researchers have started to illuminate the spiritual dimension of sexual abuse. There is an increasing interest in the relationships between spiritual well-being and psychological and physical wellness.[27] A person's spiritual world, or spirituality, involves the ultimate and personal truths that the individual holds as inviolable, providing them with meaning, hope, esteem, and belonging. It has been defined as "one's personal relationship to the sacred or transcendent, a relation that then

21. Volf, *The End of Memory*.
22. Means, *Trauma & Evil*, 4–5.
23. Shengold, *Soul Murder*, 2.
24. Doehring, *Internal Desecration*, 137. *God representation* is the term used to describe conscious and unconscious images of God.
25. Herman, *Trauma and Recovery*, 7.
26. Van der Kolk et al., *Traumatic Stress*, 573.
27. Benner, *Psychotherapy and Spiritual Tradition*.

informs other relationships and the meaning of one's own life."[28] Matters such as the quest for identity, relatedness, happiness, success, perfection, truth and justice, beauty, stimulation, and mystery, may appear to be simply psychological, but Benner claims they are psycho-spiritual matters with spiritual significance.[29] Christian spirituality, as distinct from religious and non-religious spirituality, has been defined as "a state of deep relationship with God made possible through faith in Jesus Christ and the life of the indwelling Spirit."[30]

Research indicates that there has been an inadequate focus on the psycho-spiritual dimensions of childhood sexual abuse.[31] Ganje-Fling and McCarthy maintain that the spiritual world of survivors can be seriously damaged by sexual trauma. Survivors are conflicted about relating to a powerful or determinative force; they struggle with feelings of hopelessness; they lack a sense of purpose; and they are "ambivalent about connecting to a community of believers."[32] Lemoncelli and Carey believe that unless there is "an intervention on the spiritual dimension," wounds from the psychological trauma of childhood sexual abuse cannot heal.[33]

The impact of childhood sexual abuse on spiritual functioning has been addressed in only a very limited body of research.[34] The extent of the damage to spiritual functioning through childhood sexual abuse seems to be affected by the same factors that affect psychosocial functioning: namely, the age when the abuse began, the number of abuse perpetrators, the relationship of the perpetrator(s) to the victim, and the severity of the abuse.[35] Survivors often experience a sense of spiritual disconnection and isolation, anger at God, and feelings of abandonment by God. Survivors report decreased spiritual well-being and hold more negative images of God than those without a history of sexual abuse. Furthermore, these types of spiritual struggles may lead to poor physical health and psychological well-being. For example, certain spiritual struggles (e.g., feeling punished

---

28. Sinnott, "Introduction," 199–200.
29. Benner, *Psychotherapy and Spiritual Tradition*.
30. Benner, *Psychotherapy and Spiritual Tradition*, 89.
31. Lemoncelli and Carey, "Psychospiritual Dynamics," 175–84.
32. Ganje-Fling and McCarthy, "Impact of Childhood Sexual Abuse," 253–59.
33. Lemoncelli and Carey, "Psychospiritual Dynamics," 175–84.
34. Ganje-Fling and McCarthy, "Impact of Childhood Sexual Abuse."
35. Severe abuse occurs "when traumatic stressors are repeated and prolonged, and are part of a totalitarian system" (Doehring, *Internal* Desecration, 113).

by God and abandoned by God) have been associated with poor mental health, impaired physical health, and mortality. Anger toward God and alienation from God has been associated with increased depression and anxiety.

Spiritual development occurs parallel with psychological development in a highly adaptive process. Theorists in affective, cognitive, social, and moral development have identified markers for various ages and stages. These areas develop along parallel lines and strongly influence one another.[36] Abused children long for, but can continue to feel unworthy of, real love. Attempting to make logical sense of their plight reinforces the conclusion that they deserve it. Socially, they can feel unworthy of respect and are vulnerable to being used as they continually seek to please. Rage is suppressed, as they feel they deserve what is happening, and anger toward another is thought to be morally wrong. A cycle of striving for perfection, increased awareness of imperfections, self-blame, and self-destructive behavior ensue. They are caught in a love-hate cycle; they hate the abuse, but feel they deserve it, and they long to be touched, held, and loved.

Spiritual and faith development theorists have also articulated a structure of various ages and stages in the area dealing with one's openness to the transcendent dimension. Fowler proposed six stages that occur in fixed order and represent successively more complex ways of organizing meaning in one's life.[37] These stages are formal in nature, and not characterized by any particular theological or belief content. For Fowler, faith is "an orientation of the total person, giving purpose and goal to one's hopes and strivings, thoughts and actions."[38] Severe abuse renders both psychological and spiritual development dysfunctional and arrested pre-maturely.[39]

The foundation for the developing self, which includes "appraising the meaning of information about God," is formed through implicit aspects of relationships with carers, as human beings are "ontologically relational."[40] During the early childhood stage of development, not only are representations of God formed from parental experience, but mythical notions of God are developed which are literal, one-dimensional, and anthropomorphic. As both psychological and spiritual development can be arrested at

---

36. Inhelder and Piaget, *Early Growth*.
37. Fowler, *Faith and Development*.
38. Fowler, *Faith and Development*, 14.
39. Lemoncelli and Carey, "Psychospiritual Dynamics," 175–84.
40. Miner, "Back to Basics," 119.

the age at which the abuse occurred, there is a fixation on the mythic-literal stage of spiritual development, and childhood notions and fears about God persist into adulthood.[41] The foundational belief in a world in which God is experienced predominantly as loving is not present; rather, a world in which God is experienced as absent and/or wrathful is envisioned. Imbens and Jonkers found that many survivors reported having a negative image of God as "cruel, uncaring, and punishing" in light of their abuse history.[42] Those suffering sustained abuse can

> begin to feel that only God can provide the solution. Since God does not intervene, reasoning proceeds to the conclusion that God does not care, God is powerless, and/or God is absent.[43]

Survivors are then "less likely to feel loved and accepted by God, to have a sense of trust in God, and to be involved in organized religion."[44]

However, it seems that spirituality and religion may be helpful and possibly important in the recovery process. A substantial body of research has indicated that religiousness and spirituality are associated with elevated levels of physical and mental health.[45] Furthermore, spirituality and religion can be "a potent resource" to people who are experiencing mental health problems.[46] Pargament and Saunders conclude,

> Contrary to the views of some of our professional forerunners, religion and spirituality are not contrary to mental health and mature relationships, but are vital to the very being of most of our clients. Psychologists ignore the spiritual dimension of psychotherapy to the detriment of their field and their clients.[47]

---

41. Carrie Doehring's research entitled *Internal Desecration: Traumatization and Representations of God* confirms an inter-relationship between experiences of severe abuse and God representations, 129.

42. Gall, Terry Lynn et al., "Spirituality," 102.

43. Means, *Trauma & Evil*, 27.

44. Gall et al., "Spirituality and Current Adjustment," 101–17.

45. Koenig et al., *Handbook of Religion and Health*.

46. Pargament and Saunders, "Introduction to Special Issue," 904. Pargament and Saunders refer to spirituality as "the thoughts, feelings and behaviors an individual engages in search of a relationship with *the sacred*"; and religion as "those thoughts, feelings and behaviors that are specifically related to a formally organized and identifiable religion."

47. Pargament and Saunders, "Introduction to Special Issue," 906

Recent studies suggest that religion may be a unique form of motivation, source of value and significance, contributor to mortality and health, source of coping, and source of distress.[48] Positive forms of religious coping, such as developing a relationship with God and seeking spiritual connection and support, have been related to improved mental and emotional health, lower levels of mortality, and less hostility in people struggling with major life events. While therapists often feel unequipped to deal with spiritual matters, researchers have demonstrated that survivors of sexual abuse frequently use spirituality as an important coping resource.[49] Some survivors turn to God and faith communities for support, while others are pre-existing members of churches.

The Church and Christian Ministry

The church has long been ignorant of childhood sexual abuse, and many church leaders and members have been unwilling to listen to the attempts of survivors to share childhood abuse secrets. The church is called to meet needs in the world today, so the spiritual issues of those who have been sexually traumatized need to constitute an important and relevant area of their concern. Helping victims of sexual trauma is part of God's work to touch lives through ministry in his church. Volf asserts,

> To struggle against evil, we must empathize with its victims. And to empathize with victims, we must know either from experience or from witnesses' stories what it means to hunger, thirst, shiver, bleed, grieve, or tremble in fear.[50]

The ethics of biblical community, then, insist that churches do not ignore those wounded and broken by childhood sexual abuse.

---

48. See Pargament, Magyar-Russell, and Murray-Swank, "Sacred and the Search," 665–87. Negative forms of religiousness, where God is viewed as angry, vengeful, or powerless against evil, can lead to fundamental fear, disillusionment, and distrust that shatters and reshapes one's view of God, people, and the world because they are perceived as implying harsh truths about the human condition that are ultimate, immutable, and eternal.

49. See Falsetti et al., "Treatment of Posttraumatic Stress," 252–60; Kennedy et al., "Changes in Spirituality," 322–28; Valentine and Feinauer, "Resilience Factors," 216–24.

50. Volf, *The End of Memory*, 31.

Pastoral care and healing have been, in the past, and should be today, a part of the ministry of the church.[51] Much has been written which highlights the distinctly religious origin to the *care and cure of* souls prior to the advent of modern psychology's impact on ministry and the adoption of *clinical* pastoral care paradigm. Reflecting on this rich diversity of the classical Christian tradition is an attempt to move forward in the best way possible.[52] Patton adds another paradigm, the *communal contextual*, which has emerged in both Catholicism and Protestantism, and which broadens the focus to include the caring community of clergy and laity. Patton holds that each of these paradigms is needed to rethink and carry out the pastoral care of the church at this point in history.[53] Benner suggests that a balanced and wise way forward for soul care and Christian ministry is to recover the good of the past and incorporate it with the best insights of the present.[54]

Some survivors of sexual abuse will be active in church life, possibly overly active. Some will turn to Christian spiritual beliefs and practices, desire involvement in a religious/spiritual community, and may seek church-based help. The church works to care for the needs of members through ministry, and this should include sexual abuse victims. That these survivors in churches are experiencing and covering emotional, physical, and spiritual pain, and many are desperate for healing, indicates the need to learn both to recognize them, and how to reach out to them. By learning to recognize the needs of sexual abuse victims, and then researching ways to best meet those needs, the church can become a healing place for them.

Spiritual conversion and church involvement do not remedy the devastation that abuse causes.[55] The journey of faith ordinarily moves back and forth between orientation and disorientation,[56] but the spiritual growth and healing of survivors is particularly conflictual and confusing.[57] They will continue to experience spiritual struggles in the acceptance of themselves, others, and life's experiences. Even after healing, victims may struggle to

---

51. See Allen, "What Is Church's Healing Ministry?," 46–54; Porterfield, *Healing in History of Christianity*; Ugeux, "New Quest for Healing," 22–40.

52. McNeill, *A History of the Cure*; Oates, "Holy Spirit as Counsellor," 233–45; Oates, *Presence of God*; Benner, *Surrender to Love*; Vining, *Spirit-Centered Counseling*; Boyd, *Reclaiming the Soul*; Moon and Benner, *Spiritual Direction*.

53. Patton, *Pastoral Care in Context*.

54. Benner, *Care of Souls*.

55. Schmutzer, "Theology of Sexual Abuse," 785–812.

56. Brueggemann, *Praying the Psalms*.

57. Ganje-Fling and McCarthy, "Impact of Childhood Sexual Abuse," 253–59.

process unilateral orders, unanticipated touching, authoritarian demeanor, certain jokes, and general power differentials.

Churches can play an active role in helping survivors by becoming safe environments where they can come and disclose their pain, feelings of shame, conflicts, and confusion, and find "emotional support and experiential validation."[58] One general principle for changing the abuse cycle stands out spiritually as it does psychologically: the importance of a "healthy trusting relationship." Lemoncelli and Carey say,

> When survivors experience unconditional acceptance of themselves and their feelings, fears, and beliefs about God and their parents, they are more likely to examine what is real for them rather than clinging to views that maintain the abuse cycle. Their rage must be vented, yet they must be allowed to express freely their need for these spiritual and parental relationships. Encouraging and allowing expression of the full range of emotions enables survivors to reframe parental and spiritual bonds. Also, experiencing unconditional acceptance from therapists may be survivors' only experience that demonstrates the possibility of God being able to love them that way.[59]

Churches can facilitate the process of "moving from a space of brokenness, emptiness and feelings of separation from oneself and others, to an awareness of one's infinite connection with a loving and caring Spirit."[60]

There are various spiritual ministries which can be made available through the local church to assist victims who are in the midst of spiritual struggles to aid in their process of recovery; these include counseling, prayer, spiritual formation programs, support groups, and teaching.[61] Pastoral counseling or conversation needs to be genuine dialogue involving moral reflection, mutuality, exploration, and discovery. Jackson and Sears found prayer, including litanies, psalms, and songs to be an important coping response.[62] Prayers of lament which give voice to disenfranchised grief, and psalms of assurance which provide emotional security, have

---

58. Saunders, "Posttraumatic Stress Symptom," 42.
59. Lemoncelli and Carey, "Psychospiritual Dynamics," 182.
60. Robinson, "Making the Hurt Go Away," 163.
61. One resource written for individual and group use is Allender, *The Wounded Heart*.
62. Jackson and Sears. "Implications of an Africentric Worldview."

been suggested as important spiritual resources.[63] Spiritual formation programs provide a place survivors "can face complex questions regarding the relationship between spiritual brokenness and sanctification, a person's sins and community, trauma and alertness to the Spirit."[64] Support groups can provide a place for dialogue, helping to expand understanding of self, others, and the world in a win/win encounter resulting in change. Sensitively communicated teaching on exploitation and incest can provide both advocacy and a raising of consciousness. The various spiritual disciplines assisting in self-reflection, spiritual reflection, and reflection on one's relationship with others can also be taught. Included are such disciplines as solitude, contemplative prayer, journal and autobiographical writing, and talking with one's closest friends.

Conclusion

In short, healing is a process of relationships[65] which facilitates the restoration of a person's capacity to receive and give life. Spiritual bonds are central not only to proper development but also to recovery from evil. In those people who seek help, there is a persistent and seemingly unquenchable drive for connection with another human being who will care and is willing to help. In churches where relationships are real, and business is conducted with family members, survivors can be reconnected with others in ways that are life-giving.

The next chapter will focus on understanding the activity of the Holy Spirit in spiritual healing from both the New Testament and theological literature. We will look at how biblical and theological writers have sought to understand the work of the Holy Spirit in the lives of individual believers.

---

63. Gould, "Spiritual Healing."
64. Schmutzer, "A Theology of Sexual Abuse," 11.
65. Wise, *Pastoral Psychotherapy*.

2

A BIBLICAL/THEOLOGICAL EXPLORATION OF SPIRITUAL MINISTRY

Introduction

THE TASK OF THIS present chapter is to develop an understanding of the activity of the Holy Spirit in spiritual healing from both the New Testament and theological literature. I will discuss how biblical and theological writers have sought to understand the work of the Holy Spirit in the lives of individual believers. As such, I will discuss the activity of the Holy Spirit in relation to (1) metaphors, models, and theologies of salvation in the New Testament; (2) salvation and healing; and (3) the church and ministry. In conclusion, I will indicate the availability of the Holy Spirit, as the continuing ministry and mission of Christ, for salvation which is healing.

Metaphors, Models, and Theologies of Salvation in the New Testament

The New Testament offers a rich variety of diverse images to explain the salvation available through the life, death, and resurrection of Jesus Christ. The Holy Spirit is always a gift that comes from God and testifies to the human spirit the salvation brought about through Christ. In seeking to explain what had taken place in the experience of salvation, the writers used images, metaphors, and comparisons readily understood at the time in order to integrate the message into the particular situations of the original listeners.

When a basic image can correlate the saving work of Christ with a human need, a theory of salvation is the result. The New Testament writers freely applied a variety of metaphors, or terms, that spoke to the needs of their audience. The various metaphors of salvation used addressed different situations and so gave rise to a variety of ways of conceiving salvation.

While the quest to find the most suitable image or theory of Christian salvation is an ongoing one, it seems that any soteriology of the New Testament must acknowledge that the unity of the New Testament is rooted in diversity.[1] Toynbee asserts, "the major error of all schematic theologies has been their attempt to use a non-metaphorical language in an area where nothing but metaphor is appropriate."[2] None of these metaphors are adequate in themselves, but all of them assert that Jesus makes God present in a saving way.

Scholars differ in respect to categorizing various biblical images and theories into paradigms. Some maintain that Christian salvation needs to be looked at through a smaller lens which provides for the multi-faceted richness. Some maintain that a larger lens would better acknowledge the underlying systems or models. And some would argue that a newer lens would remove the particulars of time, place, author, audience, and circumstance.

In the classic work of Gustaf Aulén, *Christus Victor*, the various biblical images and theories came to be generally categorized under three broad paradigms: Christus Victor, objective, and subjective. The Christus Victor paradigm utilizes the conflict-victory motifs of the New Testament. The central idea of this approach, according to Aulén, is "Christ—Christus Victor—fights against and triumphs over the evil powers of the world, the *tyrants* under which mankind is in bondage and suffering."[3] This developed into the ransom theory where God redeems humanity from Satan's power.

The objective model of salvation understands the work of Christ as addressing a necessary demand of God's justice. The important motifs here are vicarious suffering, sacrifice, justification, and propitiation/expiation. Theories which fall within this paradigm are the "substitutionary," "Latin," "commercial," and "Anselmian."

---

1. Dunn, *Unity and Diversity*.
2. Toynbee, *Towards the Holy Spirit*, 64.
3. Aulén, *Chritus Victor*, 4.

A Biblical/Theological Exploration

The subjective paradigm understands the primary focus of salvation to be human-ward. Jesus' work of atonement is understood to be directed at human beings and not at God. People need to be reconciled to God, and not the reverse. Subjective theories draw from reconciliation, revelatory, family-adoption and healing motifs. Peter Abelard's (1079–1142) moral influence theory and Faustus Socinus' (1539–1604) moral example theory are examples of this paradigm.

Far from limiting or grouping the images to describe the work of Christ, some want to move in the other direction. Instead of one theory of atonement or salvation, or Aulén's three broad paradigms, the scriptures affirm a multiplicity of theories. A theory must be recognized on the basis of its "basic image" and "must be able to correlate the saving power of Christ with a specific human need."[4]

Ted Peters compares and contrasts six models of the atoning work of Christ that have appeared in Christian theology.[5] He holds that these are rival interpretations of what the Bible says about the work of Christ sitting side by side in Scripture without adjudication. *Jesus as teacher of true knowledge* brings divine knowledge and wisdom into human darkness and ignorance (John 14:6). *Jesus as moral example and influence* teaches and models the life of unselfish love which is salvation. *Jesus as victorious champion and liberator* defeated sin, the devil, and death in the resurrection, and liberates people from them through the power of the Holy Spirit.[6] *Jesus as our satisfaction* fulfilled the need for cosmic justice and rendered people forgiven and righteous through his sacrifice. *Jesus as the happy exchange* constitutes salvation through an exchange between the human and divine natures where the attributes of Christ's divinity become present in his incarnation, and the attributes of his humanity become present in the divine life. *Jesus as the final scapegoat* looks at the cross and exposes our own scapegoating which has been covered with hypocritical lies.[7] Peters shows how existing paradigms of salvation can be broken down into further valid images, highlighting the theological systematization that has occurred in interpreting New Testament writings.

---

4. Schmiechen, *Saving Power*, 314.

5. Peters, "Six Ways of Salvation," 223–35.

6. This is Aulen's *Christus Victor* paradigm.

7. This is developed in light of the recent theory of scapegoating put forth by Rene Girard and is a more intense form of the moral example theory.

Driver lists ten motifs around the New Testament salvation images: conflict/victory/liberation; vicarious suffering; archetypal (representative man, pioneer, forerunner, first-born); martyr; sacrifice; expiation/wrath of God; redemption, justification; reconciliation; and adoption.[8] Green argues for the "kaleidoscopic" approach where no single view can capture the multifaceted richness of what has to be said about salvation.[9] Finlan takes a different approach altogether, reversing the shift that has happened due to Aulén's *Christus Victor*, and replaces the death of Christ and the atonement with the incarnation and the life of Christ as the center of theology.[10]

The New Testament canon was "not written as a unity or a planned, coherent body of thought."[11] The writers weren't bound by one particular interpretation but were free to apply a variety of metaphors or terms that spoke to the needs of their audience. The death of Jesus is a "historical event of such profundity that we . . . only do it violence by narrowing its meaning to one interpretation or by privileging one interpretation over all the others."[12] We can too easily make sense of the scandal of the death of God's Messiah.

When the true scandal of the cross is obscured, the rich variety of its New Testament interpretations is boycotted.[13] For early believers, the thought that God could make salvation available through the cross involved a change of worldview of colossal proportions. For the early church, the scandal of the cross was far more self-evident than its meaning. That scandal became the fertile soil of interpretative possibilities. It was a puzzle to be contemplated and a paradox to be explored.

The diverse writings of the New Testament should be seen as integrating the message of salvation into the particular situations of their original listeners. The shared tradition was interpreted and applied according to the needs of specific situations. Because the New Testament writings address diverse situations, they express their understanding of salvation differently. Sometimes the different metaphors and images used to express the process and dynamics of salvation overlap; that is, they address the same issue in different ways. The underlying issue is the salvific actions of God touching

8. Driver, *Understanding Atonement*.
9. Green, "Kaleidoscopic View," 157–96.
10. Finlan, *Problems with Atonement*.
11. Van der Watt, *Salvation in New Testament*, 505.
12. Baker and Green, *Recovering the Scandal*, 111.
13. Baker and Green, *Recovering the Scandal*.

desperate human need and, "leading to the restorations of relations, changing enmity into peace and friendship . . . [which] puts them [believers] under obligation to act according to their status."[14] This "living action" of God in the world is the Holy Spirit.[15]

Conversely, some argue that metaphors such as victory, atonement, and illumination tend to over-privilege the pertinent metaphor and lose sight of the underlying systems or models and aim to look at Christian salvation through a larger lens than metaphor. Clifford, Richard, Anatolios, and Khaled have suggested three models: prophetic, liturgical, and sapiental.[16] The prophetic model emphasizes that God is actively involved in human history in ways that constantly open up a future that leads to salvation. The liturgical model emphasizes the indwelling of God's life-giving and redeeming holiness. The sapiental model emphasizes divine self-revelation as a salvific category—God makes his ways known to humanity and the reception and enactment of this knowledge is salvation. In the New Testament, these models find their unity in the person and work of Christ.

It is further claimed that many of the traditional expressions of Jesus as the bringer of God's salvation are too removed from contemporary experience. Baker and Green maintain that the way in which the atonement is frequently and popularly expressed now tragically poses needless obstacles to twenty-first-century people and cultures.[17] This is a new kind of scandal but one that is foreign to the New Testament. Schmiechen makes the point that the church, to be effective in its mission, must recognize the variety of ways the human condition is remedied by Christ's saving power.[18] He holds that appreciating the variety of atonement models can help this occur. Haight attempted to analyze the nature of objective salvation through the experience of it. He explains that there are a variety of ways that salvation is conceived in the New Testament because the experience of Jesus as savior spread and developed unevenly in different communities with different traditions.[19]

None of these notions of salvation is adequate in themselves, but all of them assert that Jesus makes God present in a saving way. The appreciation

---

14. Van der Watt, *Salvation in New Testament*, 516.
15. Hendry, *Holy Spirit in Christian Theology*, 12.
16. Clifford and Anatolios, "Christian Salvation," 739–69.
17. Baker and Green, *Recovering the Scandal*.
18. Schmiechen, *Saving Power*.
19. Haight, "Jesus and Salvation," 225–52.

of Jesus as the medium, symbol, or sacrament of God's salvation is the genesis of the highly figurative, symbolic, and at times, mythological language of salvation. The tradition that became the New Testament is an interpretation of Jesus as savior, as is the theological development that followed based on his memory in the written text.

In attempting to interpret the experience that underlies and sustains these interpretations of Jesus, Haight overviews classical authors on salvation such as Irenaeus, Origen, Athanasius, and Gregory of Nyssa as representatives of the Greek-speaking Eastern tradition; Augustine, Anselm, and Abelard for the Latin tradition, and Luther and Calvin as Reformation theologians. This is done to develop a phenomenology of experience based on salvation theories. He then describes four distinctive characteristics of a contemporary notion of salvation which must: be something that can be experienced now, not just in the future; incorporate the world rather than escaping it; be interpreted not only individually, but also socially; and address the connection between human action and the ultimate state of things, the eschaton.

By removing the particularities of time, place, author, audience and circumstance, Haight focuses on seven themes: Jesus as the revelation of God; the experience of encountering God in Jesus; experiencing God as loving creator; the evil which holds human existence in bondage being exposed in the encounter; the radical extent of God's self-gift to human beings; salvation through Jesus showing us the way; and the resurrection hope as meeting the basic human desire for eternal life. In this way, he is attending to the texts in their past context, analyzing the transcendental or potentially universal human experience implicit in the texts, and appropriating the meaning by correlating it with present-day contexts and questions.

In response to these, the traditional experiences of salvation are reinterpreted for our age. Essentially, Jesus is salvation by being revealer. His whole person reveals a God who is present and for us and this revelation is salvific. He reveals a God whose salvation is an integral part of God's creating. While salvation and creation can be distinguished, they cannot be separated. Jesus reveals the creator is loving savior prior to creating. God saves by restoring genuine autonomy and vocation to human freedom in the world. Furthermore, Jesus makes God present for our response. The Spirit continues the presence of Christ beyond the brief span of his physical appearance and completes it by affecting its inner apprehension in people.

Regarding the development of New Testament theologies, Matera highlights the diverse ways that Paul and John understood God's revelation, the human condition, and salvation. Paul's focus was on the redemptive moment of the cross and what results from it.[20] The Johannine tradition reflects on the pre-existence and incarnation of the Word. Whereas John's Christology presents Christ as the one who reveals God to the world, Paul's Christology presents Christ as the one in whom God reveals himself to the world. God is revealed in both Johannine and Pauline Christology. For John and Paul, Christology is pre-eminently soteriology; their understandings are related to his benefits. John summarizes the benefits as life; Paul, as justification and reconciliation.

The differences in soteriological depictions are explained in their starting points. Paul begins with the redemptive death and resurrection of Christ and talks of justification and reconciliation. John begins with the incarnation and talks of the life that the Son communicates to believers. Paul focuses on the scandal of the cross and the power of the resurrection. John focuses on the life-giving revelation that the Son brings from the Father. The two cannot be harmonized, nor are meant to be. They are the results of unique experiences of Christ. Each Christology reveals something about God, the human condition, and the benefits of Christ, which the other does not, and perhaps cannot reveal. The mystery of Christ is multifaceted.

Rather than a unified teaching concerning the forms and dynamics of salvation in the New Testament, there is a collage of soteriological facets. There is such a rich texture to the soteriological landscape that it "does not lend itself into being diminished into precis form." [21] While the authors present great diversity, the unity lies in the activity of God to bring about human redemption.[22] The bringer of these inner experiences of the outward fact of Christ is the function of the Holy Spirit.

Salvation and Healing

Christian salvation is holistic, encompassing spiritual, emotional, relational, physical, and material levels of human existence. Jesus often used salvation and healing as synonymous (Matt 9:21, 22; Mark 5:23, 28, 34, 10:52; Luke 8:36, 48, 50, 17:19, 18:42; Acts 4:9, 14:9). Conradie argues the

---

20. Matera, "Christ in Theologies," 237–56.
21. Van der Watt, *Salvation in New Testament*, 505.
22. Hultgren, "Salvation," 215–22.

Christian Gospel promises a sense of comprehensive well-being and should not be reduced.[23] He posits that the various soteriological themes are related to two basic questions: "How did we get into this predicament from which we need to be saved?" (the doctrine of sin) and "What is primarily needed within this predicament?" (the doctrine of salvation).

In the New Testament and the subsequent history of Christianity, there is a rich array of metaphors that describe salvific experiences which are both rich and rooted within a particular *Sitz im Leben*. They often originated in concrete and very specific predicaments in which "salvation" was experienced. Conradie further suggests some structural differences between various soteriological concepts in the Christian tradition can be detected when it is recognized that some situations are approached by addressing the roots of the predicament in the past, some by alleviating the current impact of the predicament, and some by developing appropriate ways of averting the problem in the future.

A review of the literature on healing in the Third Wave Movement indicates their belief that,

> God's healing power is available in all aspects of life . . . Healing from spiritual sickness is better known as salvation. Healing from the effects of past hurts involves the restoration of inner peace. Healing from demonization frees the person from the control or influence of demons . . . healing from physical illness is the restoration of physical wholeness.[24]

Sin's entrance impacted the "social, psychological, emotional, environmental, and spiritual aspects of life."[25] Salvation involves not only forgiveness, reconciliation, and redemption but also healing or re-integration (Isa 53:5; Mark 2:5–12; Ps 103:2–3). In fact, healing can function as "a comprehensive soteriological concept as it can address all the models of salvation."[26]

Thomas explores the ways that John's Gospel affirms the connection between healing and salvation.[27] He argues that there are explicit associations between healing and salvation. He finds four specific and one general reference to Jesus' signs of healing (4:46–54; 5:1–18; 6:2; 9:1–41; 11:1–57)

---

23. Conradie, "Healing in Soteriological Perspective," 4.
24. Wright, "Profiles of Divine Healing," 276.
25. Wimber, *Power Evangelism*, 68–69.
26. Conradie, "Healing in Soteriological Perspective," 20
27. Thomas, "Healing in the Atonement," 23–39.

A Biblical/Theological Exploration

which reveal the holistic nature of healing and salvation from John's perspective. The relationship between the first sign, belief in Jesus, and the salvific life which Jesus brings is quite clear. The second sign entails Jesus asking a man if he wants to be whole, a term meaning more than physical healing, and including forgiveness of sins. The third indicates the close connection between healing and salvation when the man's encounter with Jesus results in more than physical sight. The final sign of healing demonstrates the relationship between healing and salvation with overt references to Jesus' resurrection.

John also takes the event of physical healing from Numbers 21:9 and focuses on the salvific dimension of the event. The statement found in John 10:10 is an indication that the superabundant life promised includes holistic healing. The word *perisson* found in the verse is only found twice previously in John and in both cases in the pericope of the feeding of the five thousand. Clearly, Thomas believes, the word has the purpose of emphasizing superabundance, in other words, holistic healing.

Health is a physical, environmental, psychological, social, moral and spiritual concept. It includes inner-healing, forgiveness, a rebuilding of broken relationship, reciprocity, renewed fellowship, cosmic harmony and a return to wholeness. Healing is a "restoration of well-being, in body, mind and spirit,"[28] where well-being or wholeness is understood as movement toward harmony with oneself, others, the material universe, and with God; it is "salvation and peace."[29] When one symbol of salvation, such as forgiveness of sins, overshadows the others, as has occurred, then the notion of forgiveness of sins is deemed sufficient to address the immediate consequences of sin, and the need for a victory over the evil consequences of human sin is sidelined.[30]

Warrington shows why and how the letter of James provides guidelines for healing praxis to be undertaken by members of the local church on behalf of others who may be suffering from varied forms of weakness. The guidelines provide a pathway to wholeness and healing in their fullest sense: a potential harmony of the physical, emotional, mental and spiritual aspects of a person. Warrington points out that the Greek terms translated "sick" in the passage are used in many different settings to identify a range

---

28. Taylor, *Sent to Heal*, 9.

29. Potter, "Healing and Salvation," 333.

30. Conradie points out that this is what has happened in the context of evangelical theologies.

of weaknesses. Three major encapsulations contain the major common meanings from eighty-one verses; there are weaknesses of a spiritual/moral nature, a physical nature, and a general nature.[31] He adds that early church writings reveal a similar variety where context is often the determining factor.

Furthermore, he points out that the terms used to describe the restoration process, namely, "save," "raise" and "heal," are also used with a variety of meanings depending upon the context.[32] With regard to "save," the identity of the salvation is determined by the situation from which the sufferer is rescued. The terms "raise" and "heal" are also variously determined. Warrington maintains that as these words are capable of receiving a number of interpretations, James is providing pastoral guidance for a comprehensive range of weaknesses in order to provide restoration and wholeness.[33] If the reason for a person's suffering is related to sin, as it sometimes is, then forgiveness is available with confession by the perpetrators.

A comprehensive look at Christianity and healing shows that healing has persisted "over time and across cultural spaces" as "a defining element of Christianity" and "a major contributor to Christianity's endurance, expansion and success."[34] Jesus' acts of healing and exorcism recorded in the Gospels are received as miracles throughout Christian thought. Porterfield moves through time from the early church to the present and indicates that various facets of healing have advanced the spread of Christianity throughout the world, and that different concepts of healing have influenced Christianity within various time periods and varying geographical localities.[35]

---

31. Warrington, "James 5:14–18," 346–49.

32. Warrington, "James 5:14–18," 350–51.

33. Regarding James' recommendation for the use of oil for anointing, Warrington thinks he intended to link the therapeutic qualities of oil with the symbolic characteristics in Jewish culture: the presence of the Spirit, restoration, a new beginning, prosperity, goodness, purity, friendship, love eternal life, joy, etc., resulting in the sufferer feeling secure and cared for by friends and God.

34. Porterfield, *Healing in History*, 19.

35. Porterhouse discusses the works of Hildegard of Bingen, Meister Eckhart, Thomas a Kempis, Ignatius, John Calvin, Albert Schweitzer, John Wesley, and Aimee Semple McPherson to indicate that a healing emphasis has adjusted to different historical periods and cultural contexts. She also examines subjects such as baptism as a healing victory over evil, medieval exorcism, the Christian medical missionary movement, the Taiping Rebellion in China, the independent Harrist Church of Africa, Pentecostalism, political healing in South Africa, the placebo effect, and present-day technological medicine.

Kydd explores both the healing ministry of Jesus and healing in Christian history. After focusing on the healing ministry of Jesus, he concludes that healing the sick was a part of the bigger picture, the kingdom of God. He then identifies six models of healing throughout the history of the church: confrontational, intercessory, reliquarial, incubational, revelational and soteriological. Kydd presents the "confrontational" model where

> Healing is seen as part of God's overarching program, in which he has become active not only in human affairs but in the destiny of the whole universe. By this action, God issued a direct challenge to Evil.[36]

Support is drawn from some church fathers.[37] Kydd also assesses Blumhardt's ministry and concludes that he held the same conviction as the church fathers. Blumhardt's eschatology, Christology and pneumatology all led him to his battle cry: "Jesus is Victor!"[38] Kydd places Wimber, whose understanding of the kingdom of God is based on Ladd's "already-not yet" hypothesis, in this model.[39]

The adherents of the "intercessory" model believe that "health can be restored by God through the intervention of one or other of the saints."[40] He examines the apocryphal Acts of the Apostles to explain how and why people came to believe that these great "agents of the miraculous" could provide intercession from beyond the grave. Brother Andre of Saint Joseph's Oratory in Quebec is presented as an example of one who began praying for the sick in the latter part of the nineteenth century and his intercession

---

36. Kydd, *Healing Through Centuries*, 19.
37. Irenaeus, Tertullian, Cyprian, Origen, and Lactantius.
38. Johann Christoph Blumhardt (1805–1880) was a German Lutheran theologian. In 1842, he had to deal with one of his parishioners, a young woman who suffered from a severe nervous disorder and whose household was visited with strange psychic phenomena. After two months of pastoral care and reverent hesitation, discovering that he had no wisdom or power that could help, he and the girl prayed together: "Lord Jesus, help us. We have watched long enough what the devil does; now we want to see what the Lord Jesus can do." This prayer-battle continued for almost two years without change—the situation deteriorating, if anything. Finally came the moment of crisis. At a point when Blumhardt's prayer and the girl's trouble were at a pitch, the girl's sister in a strange voice suddenly uttered the cry, "Jesus Is Victor!"—and it was all over. The latter became a servant in the Blumhardt household and lived there the rest of her life; but she was never troubled again.
39. Kydd, *Healing Through Centuries*, 49. See Ladd, *Presence of Future*, 149.
40. Kydd, *Healing Through Centuries*, 61.

is believed to have continued after his death in 1937. Martin of Tours is another example.

The "reliquarial" model is described as the approach which associates healing with the remains of bodies or objects which came into contact with a saint. He examines records from the mid-fourth century until the late fifteenth century, including writings by Ambrose and Augustine.

The "incubational" model includes the healing home at Mannedorf begun by Dorothea Trudel in the late nineteenth century and the Pentecostal retreat center, Morija, at Yverdon-les-Bains. Here, the emphasis is on giving people time to respond to God and giving God time to move. Similarly, Warrington notes that for James, *the prayer of faith* is the determining factor in the healing process. He believes the prayer is best identified as knowledge of God's will for a particular situation when no scriptural guidance is given. This knowledge results in a confident expectation that the outcome, as revealed, will result. Such a prayer is offered by one who has taken the time to tap God's resource of wisdom and appropriate it to the particular situation. Warrington quotes MacNutt and Nel who support a healing praxis where prayer takes place over a period of time.[41] Warrington also explains why leaders together should be involved in this prayer, why they are to pray in the name of the Lord, and why Elijah is a fitting example of this kind of prayer.

The "revelational" model includes the twentieth century healing evangelists, William Branham and Kathryn Kulman. The final model is the "soteriological," and here Kydd looks at the ministry of Oral Roberts.[42] He traces the Pentecostal belief of divine healing in the atonement from its roots in the holiness-healing tradition.

Kydd affirms diversity in healing practice, calls for verification, and concludes that healing arises out of a relationship with God, and that room needs to be left for the mystery of God, in order to avoid formulaic explanations and no one methodology is seen as prescriptive.

Ugeux sees a convergence between the current increased interest and quest for spirituality in Western society and the demand for health. Many today do not accept that a spiritual journey can be beneficial without a journey of human and personal development. People also want to be valued as unique individuals and treated holistically rather than mechanistically. He

---

41. See MacNutt, *Healing Through Prayer*; Nel, *The Way to Healing*.

42. Citing Oral Roberts as the only example is unfortunate as many in the Pentecostal movement would not see him as necessarily stereotypical.

sees this as positive but mentions some risks, one of which is that becoming one's perfected self is not the same as conversion. The criteria for spiritual maturity are: "the growth of interior freedom, a greater gratuity (graciousness) in relationships, the acceptance of reality (of what we cannot change), and what is specific to Christianity, the configuration to Christ."[43] Nonetheless, this presents an invitation to Christianity to "do a work of inculturation that not only keeps in mind contemporary developments but also is accompanied by an authentic interdisciplinary discernment,"[44] so Christian communities can become communities of healing and reconciliation, acknowledging the source of human "liberation" and "fulfillment" coming from the God of love through the sacrifice of Christ.[45]

In response to the question of what it means to heal, Ugeax looks at some groups coming from the Catholic charismatic renewal movement such as: The House of Lazarus, where a distinction is made between spiritual, medical and psychotherapeutic work; The Community of the Beatitudes, where a psycho-spiritual approach focuses on somatic, psychological and spiritual dimensions together; and Simone Pacot who offers sessions for "the evangelization of the depths." The faculty research department of theology at Toulouse, which Ugeax directs, sets out to find the theologies underlying these healing practices. The research concerns conceptions of health and healing and their relationship to sin, the taking of responsibility in the face of evil, the interpretation of "original sin," and the relationship between healing and salvation and their definitions. For Ugeax the spiritual life is inseparable from the affective and bodily life. He considers that when Christians really live "the law of the Incarnation," they have their own way of being holistic. The more human a person becomes, the more they become divine. The Christian understanding of maturing as healing is always situated in community.

The Church and Ministry

As mentioned, the Gospel accounts of Christ's healing miracles present a profusion of different forms of healing. Luke records the early church healing as Jesus did and intends these healings to demonstrate the authority of Jesus in the life of the church. These healings demonstrate that, in spite of

43. Ugeux, "New Quest for Healing," 30.
44. Ugeux, "New Quest for Healing," 22.
45. Ugeux, "New Quest for Healing," 40.

his ascension and bodily absence, Jesus is actually present, as is evidenced by the healings involving Peter, Paul, Stephen, Phillip, and Ananias. Luke is not providing a methodology of healing, nor indicating that many were involved in this ministry, or that it was available to all believers, rather "his aim is to demonstrate that in the healing accounts recorded, Jesus is the central influence and he paints him into the picture."[46]

This does not mean that the miracles are the creation of the author who wants to fashion the apostles in the likeness of Jesus, nor do these healings demonstrate how these men emulated Jesus. A christological reason supports the healing parallels. They demonstrate the presence and person of Jesus. Jesus is still resourcing the ministry of the church. Warrington offers three reasons in support of this. First, the healings affirm the messengers as those entrusted with announcing a new era of salvation, as they did in Jesus' ministry—healings are a foretaste of the coming Kingdom. Second, the healings are the launching pads for each new phase of the mission announced in 1:8 which Luke reminds his readers in 1:1 is a continuation of Jesus' ministry. Third, the healings confirm that they are healers in the mold of Jesus. Warrington says that while it is inappropriate to adopt a methodology from Acts, the healings in Acts should encourage the church to still believe that healings can occur.

Jesus, as the continuing mission of God in the world, issues forth the church that receives the Spirit of Pentecost, thus becoming an empowered and sent people. Anderson says,

> The continued presence and work of the Holy Spirit constitute the praxis of Christ's resurrection. This means that the truth of the resurrection is not only the fact of a historical event but the presence and power of a resurrected person, Jesus Christ.[47]

Luke-Acts establishes the inseparable nature of the relationship between Jesus as the Son of God and the giver of the Holy Spirit; and equally, the inseparable nature of the relationship between the Holy Spirit and the Church as the believing community. The Holy Spirit imparts to people the knowledge of their unity with Christ and one another. Paul speaks of "the fellowship of the Holy Spirit" (2 Cor 13:14) and "fellowship in the Spirit" (Phil 2:1). Today, the broken-hearted, wounded suffering can hear Jesus

---

46. Warrington, "Acts and Healing Narratives," 191.
47. Anderson, *Ministry on the Fireline*, 30.

A Biblical/Theological Exploration

speak to them a word of peace, comfort, hope, healing, and understanding through the church empowered by the Holy Spirit.

The ministry of Christ is transferred through the Spirit to his disciples in every generation as the body of Christ and agent of the Kingdom of God. The church discovers and enters more into ministry as it discovers and enters more into Christ's ministry. Ministry, then, is the continuing work of Christ through the Spirit in the church to fulfill God's mission of bringing humankind to wholeness, that is, into harmonious communion with God and each other, into true community.

Healing, wholeness, peace and harmony do not come about by the application of methods discovered in the Bible, but through the presence and power of the resurrected Jesus working through the Spirit to fulfill God's mission. LaCugna refers to this divine movement of God in human history when she says that, "Everything comes from God through Christ, in the Spirit, and everything returns to God through Christ in the Spirit."[48]

Christians then are to be healers who proclaim and demonstrate a total gospel of forgiveness and healing, healers of the whole person, and healers in a healing community. Anderson says, "there is no Christ for the world other than the Christ who is present in the form of the Holy Spirit indwelling persons and empowering them."[49] Many have argued that Western-influenced churches have abandoned the healing mandate of Christ to the medical, psychological, and other professionals, and that is why these churches are at such a low ebb.[50]

While a whole person approach to health and human development is greatly needed, it has been neglected by both Western medicine and Christianity. Fichter confronts the sufficiency of today's physicians to care for the spiritual dimensions of patients in promoting whole person health.[51] He provides evidence that whole-person care is a major deficiency in America's health care system.[52] Furthermore, Western notions of a "spirit-body" or

---

48. La Cugna, *God for Us*, 356.

49. Anderson, *Ministry on the Fireline*, 44.

50. McNeill, *A History of the Cure*; Oden, *Care of Souls*; Benner, *Care of Souls*; Boyd, *Reclaiming the Soul*; Allen, "What is the Church's Healing Ministry?"; Moon and Benner, *Spiritual Direction*; Kelleman, *Soul Physicians*.

51. Fichter, *Healing Ministries*.

52. Fichter collated responses from twenty health professionals including doctors, surgeons, psychiatrists, catholic sisters and priests, chaplains, pastoral care directors, professors, directors of nursing and pastoral care, nurses, psychiatric nurses, social workers, and chaplains—many of which were qualified and experienced in more than one

a "soul-body" dualism have side-tracked the church from a theology of healing and from a notion of wholeness as central to Christian ministry. Genesis tells us when God created Adam and breathed into his nostrils, he became a living *nephesh*, or soul. This identifies the human individual as a totality rather than a body with a compartmentalized soul.

There have been numerous recent attempts to re-appreciate classical Christian soul care, and filter and go beyond its recent preoccupation with popular psychotherapies and the other social sciences, in order to find a contemporary Christian, biblical and culturally informed approach to helping, healing and transforming people in real and great need.[53] There are a growing number of voices arguing that church communities have something unique to offer the world in its ministry of healing.[54] There are certain elements of a local congregation that are not found in a secular environment: a fellowship formed by the Holy Spirit (Eph 2:18–22); gifts of the Spirit for ministry; proclamation of the gospel as the good news of grace; teaching for Christian growth; and most importantly, prayer as our means of access to God. These can enable churches to be organic, therapeutic, and total care communities where each person is equally valued, and where people can heal in community with others.

The beginning of the twenty-first century has seen many churches worldwide making an effort to reclaim the healing ministry of the church by returning to the practice of establishing healing ministries.[55] This is built on the convictions that all Christians can become agents of healing in each other's lives, that this can be accomplished by incorporating prayer for healing and transparent relationships with one another, and that the church needs to become a context where healing can occur. The church has been a place of healing and health since its inception, and Jesus modelled this role effectively. The theological significance of the miracles of Jesus is that they bear witness to God's intention to restore wholeness to all people and

---

of these areas. They were mainly Catholic, but also Episcopalian, Jewish, Lutheran, and Presbyterian. He maintains the only generalization that fits all the responses is a holistic concept of healthcare. Each of them saw the spiritual dimension of health care alongside physical, mental, and psychological care. They all agreed that tending the sick includes religious consolation.

53. McNeill, *A History of the Cure*; Oden, *Care of Soul*; Oates, *The Presence of God*; Rediger, "From Sickness to Well-Being."

54. Allen, "What is the Church's Healing Ministry?"; Crabb, *Connecting*.

55. Granberg-Michaelson, "Reclaiming Healing Ministry," 134–36.

all creation. They also imply that the person who receives healing will, in gratitude, seek to engage in covenant living.

Rediger holds that the clergy ought to see themselves as ministers of health and healing. He urges churches to develop health and healing ministries within their congregation and provides reasons why they should do so. First, "health and healing are part of our salvation."[56] Second, "Jesus spent much of his earthly ministry engaged in healing and teaching about body-mind-spirit health."[57] Third, until recently the church has been a place of healing and health care. Fourth, it is now apparent that a critical element has been left out in modern medicine and psychology, namely spirituality. He notes that a trend toward health and healing ministries is emerging which he says presents powerful witness to the gospel. While the Pentecostal movement has held healing to be part of the gospel, Theron pleads for a new praxis-theory in the healing ministry of Pentecostal churches to enable participation in a better and more biblically-based way. He advocates a shift from the atonement as the sole basis for healing to other bases, such as the "already-not yet" nature of the in-breaking of the Kingdom of God, in order to develop a healthy healing ministry.[58]

Conclusion

In conclusion, Luke says, "God anointed Jesus of Nazareth with the Holy Spirit and with power" (Acts 10:38), meaning the Holy Spirit came upon Jesus to enable him to fulfill his ministry and mission. At every point in the ministry of Jesus, we see the activity of the Holy Spirit. The same Holy

---

56. Rediger, "Ministries of Health and Healing," 14.

57. Rediger, "Ministries of Health and Healing," 14.

58. Theron, "Towards a Practical Theological Theory," 49–65. Areas Theron considers important for further consideration are: the discrepancy between the practice of Pentecostals and their original theology; the question of whether some believers feel safer and more cared for in the secular world than in the church; big meetings replacing the congregational setting as the place for healing; the question of those who are not instantaneously healed; the care of those who suffer sickness over a prolonged period; the effect of the demonic upon believers; the influence of current Western worldview upon Pentecostals and healing; the importance of the Eucharist in the healing ministry; the place and practice of the anointing of oil for healing; the place and practice of the gifts of the Spirit alongside the gift of healing and healing ministry; the role of a caring and loving church in the healing of a person; the place of healing teams in the ministry of the local church; terminological issues; prayer for societal healing; and the influence of non-Pentecostal Christian healing beliefs and practices.

Spirit was promised to those who repented and believed after Jesus' ascension (Acts 2:38). When the early church experienced the in-breaking of the Spirit at Pentecost, his presence and power were clearly identifiable. This "in-breaking" of the Spirit challenged the way things were and ushered in the new.

Similarly, the Spirit is still active today in the lives of Christian believers in ways which we can identify. While Christ himself remains hidden and beyond human physical sight today, nonetheless we can plainly see his works and gifts affected by the Spirit and made manifest in the world, the church, and the lives of Christians. In this, we are to look for "the footprints of Christ's presence."[59] The Spirit still works by "in-breaking" but also works by "growing" the good things that are already happening in this world. Crisis and process are not incompatible. Accounts of spiritual healing point to the God of whose kingdom they are signs. They reflect the ongoing transformation of human life under the divine initiative.

---

59. Oden, *Pastoral Theology*, 193.

3

BIOGRAPHICAL AND HEALING NARRATIVES

Chapter 1 emphasized that the devastation of childhood sexual abuse involves a spiritual dimension and requires spiritual restoration and sought to understand this further in the context of Christian ministry within the local church. Chapter 2 focused on the activity of the Holy Spirit in spiritual healing from both the New Testament and theology. This third chapter provides the biographical and healing narratives of seven childhood sexual abuse victims who have experienced spiritual healing.

The descriptions of the journeys of the seven recovered victims from woundedness to recovery were recorded, transcribed, reflected upon, and interrogated in order to arrive at findings that comprehended the experience of the participants. This began with two ninety-minute interview sessions for each participant. Each first interview commenced with the participant reflecting on and discussing their spiritual journey. Once they felt they had said all they could, I asked whether we could now talk about the sexual abuse. The second interview involved each participant reflecting on and discussing their healing journey. The second interview, in most cases, began with unsolicited comments around further reflections that had surfaced between the interviews.[1] The transcriptions of the available data was reflected upon and analyzed using the phenomenological method.[2]

Introducing the Participants

Liam

Liam was actively involved in the Catholic Church until the age of fourteen when his family joined an independent Pentecostal church. He made a commitment to Christ at seven years of age and was baptized in the Spirit at nine.[3] Liam now works part-time as a pastor. He was sexually abused by his father, who was the pastor of their church, for ten years from the age of thirteen under the guise of ministry and education. Other leaders in the church were similarly abused. When the associate pastor opened up to the eldership, the full impact and implications began to be recognized. Liam was relieved to find that his life had been abnormal. A volunteer Christian counselor assisted the family. The beginning of real healing came when a trusted pastor encouraged him to forgive the perpetrator. Forgiving unburdened him and renewed a positive outlook. Freedom from his father's control renewed his personal strength. Prayer counseling brought further healing and convinced him that God brings healing gradually and at the right time.

---

1. See Appendix 1 for the interview questions. The beginning of the first interview was admitted to be difficult by each participant. Together with the conviction that this was something they ought to be doing, there was an almost overwhelming sense of vulnerability. Later, several participants indicated that one wrong response from myself would have caused them to literally get up and run. However, at the beginning of the second interview most participants indicated the benefits they felt from being able to reflect upon the whole story of their abuse from where they are at now. Several of the females were pleased that they had been able to open up to a male. One sent a Christmas card indicating how affirmed she was in being able to tell her story to a male pastor and feel listened to.

2. See Appendix 2 for a brief overview of the phenomenological methodological approach employed. Phenomenology, as a philosophical theory, generated in the first half of the twentieth century by Edmund Husserl, Martin Heidegger, Maurice Merleau-Ponty, and Hans-George Gadamer. It focuses on and seeks to understand, in a deep and rich way, the meaning of human experiences which are held to be pregnant with potential and actual meaning, and is widely used in social science, health care, psychology, theology, and pastoral care.

3. *The baptism with the Holy Spirit* is understood here to be a separate and distinct experience occurring at some point after regeneration.

Biographical and Healing Narratives

Sophia

After her mother left, Sophia moved to stay with her grandmother. Her grandmother had been recently converted and read the Bible to her. At six years of age, she returned with her siblings to the family home, but it was more like living with strangers. She dreaded family gatherings which included children and adults from first and second marriages. There was excessive drinking and the males got gropey.[4] The children had to assume responsibility for the household. At eleven she was sexually abused by a relative.[5]

Church involvement helped her realize that her family life was abnormal and ungodly. That helped her to stop the abuse escalating. Experiencing Christian homes caused her to resent the deprivation of her own family.[6] She returned to church at thirty-two when her life started to fall apart. The presence and power of the Holy Spirit impacted her. The hurt child within began to find words to describe what had happened. Healing lessened the painful memories and the raw places. Sophia considers that without supernatural intervention, she could have ended up in prison.

Emma

Emma was molested by her father from eight years of age. Her mother did not believe it was occurring. At thirteen, her doctor wanted her to report the abuse, but her mother objected. At fourteen, she stayed with her Christian grandmother for twelve months. They read the Bible together and she felt loved. Emma decided on Christ at fourteen years of age but stopped attending church at seventeen because of other priorities. She recommitted her life to Christ and returned to church at thirty. It was an encounter with God in a church service that initiated her healing. She suddenly saw herself covered in blackness. The Spirit told her this was due to her abuse.

Telling her pastor about the abuse marked the beginning of her journey toward being able to forgive and find healing. Emma learned to listen to God and allow him to correct her negative and self-justifying thinking. She found God often spoke to her by reading the Bible. She was helped to

---

4. Before the age of ten she had experienced inappropriate touching and tongue-kissing.

5. The relative kissed her, touched her, and penetrated her vagina with his fingers.

6. During this time she was anorexic and bulimic.

grow in confidence through several close church leaders, both female and male. She allowed her old perceptions to be replaced and found her true identity and security through God's acceptance of her into his family.

Julian

It was while visiting relatives to support them through some trouble that Julian experienced being touched by his seventeen-year-old cousin in ways that he had not experienced before. Julian was eleven years of age and particularly vulnerable as his father had recently passed away. The sexual encounters occurred about a dozen times over a two-year period. He felt helpless to resist his cousin's enticements.

At seventeen years of age, Julian was converted to Christ through being invited to a youth group and church. For the first time, Julian felt he was finding some answers and experiencing relationship at a deeper level. While his conversion brought some freedom and release, it didn't bring complete healing. Julian still suppressed what he felt inside. He had his guard up continually and responded to external events by drawing from "a massive warehouse" inside of appropriate responses. He was afraid that opening up would mean rejection.

Julian first spoke about the abuse to his mother when he was twenty-five. Healing came from a deeper experience of God's love. He attributes feeling safe enough for things to surface and be healed was due to the Holy Spirit as Comforter.

Adam

Adam grew up with Christian parents and grandparents and served as an altar boy and in the choir. At twelve years of age, he was sexually abused by a friend of the family. The abuse occurred over a two-month period and involved pornography and masturbation. Later a second abusive experience extended over three years involving inordinate affection from his rector who had become his substitute father and spiritual mentor. On one occasion the rector sought, unsuccessfully, to advance the level of affection between them to a sexual encounter. At thirty-seven, Adam, an ordained minister, was baptized in the Holy Spirit and his church became involved in the Charismatic Renewal. This enabled him to forgive both his perpetrators and himself. Later Adam was involved with some intensive prayer counseling with a spiritual director where issues were revisited and resolved through confession, prayer, and a renewal of biblical and spiritual thinking.

Chloe

Chloe's parents were Exclusive Brethren missionaries. As a child, she was fully involved in all church activities including meeting on Sunday for most of the day and regular, and sometimes all-night, prayer meetings. When Chloe contracted hepatitis, she was looked after by a nearby family from church. During that time, she was sexually abused by one of the sons who was also an elder in the church. The abuse involved inappropriate levels of affection and masturbation. This continued over a period of five years, every time her family paid them a visit. It left her with numerous problems including major trust issues. At nineteen, Chloe attended a bible college where she asked Christ into her life.

At thirty-five years of age, Chloe came under the overwhelming influence of the Holy Spirit in a church service.[7] The experience continued for three days. It was after three days of a "movie-camera experience" of remembering her abuse in vivid detail that God brought healing. Chloe came out of the experience with the memories, but "no pain." Chloe is now an ordained minister and qualified counselor.

Scarlett

Scarlett started going to church with her family at six years of age. At around eleven, she queried whether she wanted anything to do with her father's God as he had sexually abused her from the age of six or seven. The abuse continued for thirteen or fourteen years on at least a weekly basis. It involved inappropriate touching and talk, which she calls verbal pornography, and was intended to break down her resistance. It wasn't until she was eighteen that she found out her father wasn't a Christian but went to church because "all good people went to church."

---

7. Chloe refers to this experience of the Holy Spirit as *the Toronto Blessing*, a term coined to describe the revival and resulting phenomena reported to have occurred at the Toronto Airport Vineyard church.

She understands her born again time to be in her third year of high school, and she was baptized at seventeen. At thirty-eight, she felt the Holy Spirit tell her to commence prayer counseling and that continued for three years. Before her healing, Scarlett experienced panic attacks, engaged in negative self-talk, and had problems with emotional and sexual intimacy. Her healing included recovery from all these and more. Her healing consisted in moments of revelation which enabled her to step up to a new level, followed by a steady process of growth.

The Interpretative Themes

Forty-one interpretative themes were identified which have been assigned under the following chapter headings: Lifeworld, Woundedness, Faith Community, Healing, and Holy Spirit.

Table 3.1

4	5	6	7	8
LIFEWORLD	WOUNDEDNESS	FAITH COMMUNITY	HEALING	HOLY SPIRIT
dysfunctionality and damage	vulnerability, manipulation, and control	spiritual foundations	remembering and understanding	the flame of the Spirit
deprivation and disempowerment	internal damage	encouraging influences	naming abuse	interventions and interruptions
disillusionment with religion	inner and outer worlds	personal and spiritual growth	disclosing abuse	revelation and change
conversion and change	images of God	cultivating the spiritual life	depth and need	event and process
Christian heritage	uncovering wounds	community and identity	facilitators to healing	infilling of the Spirit
discovering God	rising emotions	mixed church experiences	inhibitors and relapses	guidance and counseling
relationship with God	oversexualization	counseling and prayer	trust and safety	overwhelming help from the Spirit
faith and calling		ministerial life and experience	forgiveness and healing	the Spirit and Christ
			identity and purpose	
			healing and wholeness	

In the table above, the content of each chapter is laid out under its heading and interpretative themes.

Conclusion

In this chapter, I have introduced each of the seven recovered victims who were interviewed by including a biographical/healing narrative for each. I have indicated the interpretative themes provided by the analysis and explication of the interviews. I have listed the five related headings that the forty-one interpretative themes feed into. These themes will form the substance of the next five chapters.

4

THE WORLD AS THE CONTEXT FOR THE ACTIVITY OF THE HOLY SPIRIT

Introduction

LIVED EXPERIENCE MUST PROVIDE the starting point in addressing spiritual healing and the activity of the Holy Spirit. This chapter will provide the overall background or horizon within which these individual experiencers find themselves. Here, we will attend to their giving definition to their own existence in the midst of their lifeworld. My intention is to provide a description of their responses to early experiences, that is, perceptions once lived through and now stored in the memory of their physical circumstances, and then explore those experiences for depth of meaning.

The relevant interpretative themes, as outlined in the previous chapter, will be addressed. These are: "dysfunctionality and damage," "deprivation and disempowerment," "disillusionment with religion," "conversion and change," "Christian heritage," "discovering God," "relationship with God," and "faith and calling."

Dysfunctionality and Damage

Emma

There are large parts of Emma's early years for which she has no memory. What little she recalls is all bad. God was not a part of her upbringing at all. Her father had sexual intercourse with Emma from eight years of age. It occurred while her mother was in the house. The frequency of the abuse increased around eleven years of age when no one would listen to her. Her mother accused her of lying. She had been placed in the abnormal role of "the other woman in the house." She was bewildered over her mother's unwillingness to listen or care. When she was thirteen, a doctor's report showed the full physical damage incurred by the abuse, but no intervention occurred.

As a child, she had no comprehension of what was happening to her, only that it wasn't normal. She learned to cope with the abuse and even use it to manipulate to her own ends. She avoided beatings for getting home late by providing sexual favors. While feeling her life was abnormal she was incapable of interpreting how abnormal it was. The abnormality was reinforced at thirteen when her brother finally ran away. She was confused and terrified. The sheer physical size of her father increased the horror of the abuse. On one occasion she resisted being raped by screaming when her friend arrived. This was the first time she had resisted in this way and it helped her understand the wrongness of her background.

Emma presented a façade of happiness and fun to her friends while not allowing them to come to her house. Behind the façade was a hatred for her home. The noise and aggression of the house environment had a detrimental effect on her progress at school. She knew her assuming responsibility for the family was inappropriate and wrongly placed. The notion of a childlike dependence and lack of responsibility was completely foreign to her.

Emma later understood that what had taken place was both deception and robbery. She was horrified by the realization that she could have become pregnant by her father. Anger and unforgiveness affected her at a level that was not immediately noticeable.

The World as the Context

Deprivation and Disempowerment

Sophia

The culture of Sophia's family for generations had involved gambling, drinking, and violence. Her relatives were co-dependent as a group. She recalls family parties as extremely negative experiences where the adult conversation was filled with helplessness and hopelessness. Their animosity toward each other was expressed in negative attitudes and emotional outbursts.

While Sophia experienced abuse as the norm during childhood, she now sees that she was disempowered significantly through the way her parents communicated with her. Her opinions were not listened to and not valued. The constant interrogation of the children about times out of the house caused them to lie to escape punishment. Parental discipline was not motivated by love but a desire to control. The parents told the children all they had was because of them. She recalls as a child regularly experiencing nightmares. She believes her home environment would cause a person to be emotionally erratic and unstable.

From her Christian teaching, she understood she was to respect her relatives, but found it difficult when they didn't respect appropriate boundaries. Her personal space was not respected at all and was infringed upon constantly. Her experiences of physical contact with adult family members lacked affection, affirmation, and good intentions. The physical contact experienced from adults was in the form of wrongly motivated punishment and sexual abuse. What her parents described as a rebellious attitude was actually depression, a way of detaching emotionally from the ungodly environment of the family home.

Sophia realized, as a child, that her family life was ungodly and hurtful to God. But it was in her teen years that she realized how deprived her life actually had been. She then became resentful and felt trapped that nothing would change. When she was finally asked to leave the family home, it was both a welcomed thing and a further sense of rejection.

Disillusionment with Religion

Chloe

Chloe was brought up in a family where God came first in everything and there was a strong emphasis on religious activities. Church was a regular part of their life and the children were included in all religious activities. She remembers a real intensity relating to activities such as learning the Scriptures. Her knowledge of the Bible was extensive, but impersonal and academic. She also remembers becoming aware of some hypocrisy in the Christian community. She wondered why there was an obvious lack of joy in her church compared to some other people of non-Christian faiths.

Chloe understands now that her parents had been schooled in, and she had been brought up in, a legalistic form of Christianity. She was taught to obey God through fear of punishment. Her early Christian experience was governed by rules. She chastised herself for her misdemeanors as self-punishment was preferable to punishment by God. Her religious background was a real disincentive to being involved in Christian service of any kind, and so a later personal call to ministry took a long time to accept. She now understands that conversion to Christianity is not the same as conversion to Christ.

Conversion and Change

Julian

Julian attended church for years before a message penetrated his heart and he was converted. It was the beginning of experiencing some good things deeply. There was a new-found love for people, and a simple confidence in God and the Bible, which for him became personally fortifying. His new faith took precedence in everything.

Having come to Christ, Julian initially felt his whole life would change, but conversion didn't bring complete healing. It brought assurance of forgiveness, but it didn't deal with the issues related to the sexual abuse. He still felt he needed to maintain an acceptable image and not open up about problems. Christianity as essentially right performance didn't seem to work. He couldn't understand why the expected change and healing hadn't happened. He didn't seek help because he was afraid of rejection. He now understands there was a lack of insight into what coming to Christ really meant.

Disillusionment with failed formulas for change led to an openness to new perspectives. Having come to the end of himself resulted in the openness to listen to God and be open to change. Really listening to God only came after all explanations and solutions had been exhausted.

The World as the Context

Christian Heritage

Adam

Adam moved home and schools so many times as a child that his schoolwork suffered as a result. His parents "lived together apart." Christianity had been a part of his family for at least three generations. There had always been church involvement. While growing up with knowledge of Jesus and the Holy Spirit, he was converted as a youth and experienced a fresh desire to read the Bible. Adam understood Jesus to be his friend, the person he could open up to, the person who sacrificed his life for him, and someone he had always admired above all others. Still today, it is Jesus Christ that commands his greatest admiration and love because of his salvation and friendship. He had an early desire to serve as a minister. Later, God spoke to him regarding a call to ordained ministry

Discovering God

Chloe

Chloe was challenged by, and pondered over, the language of personal faith used by some Christians. She remembers wondering how what she saw in the Bible could become personal for her. When she did receive Christ, she was challenged to share her newly-found faith openly and immediately. She quickly professed to others that she had experienced a rebirth through the Holy Spirit. Now she understands that to be in Christ involves a personal surrender, rebirth, and an ongoing willingness for self-sacrifice.

Chloe now understands Jesus to be the savior of all, and the Holy Spirit to be God-living-in-her through her acceptance of the person and work of Jesus. That understanding gave her a greater sense of self-worth. It also enabled her to step into the opportunities for Christian service that she believed God was providing. One such area where a strong desire developed was in helping women to be at peace with themselves and trusting God's work in their lives. Chloe's conversion led to addressing some areas where she felt conviction for past actions.

Relationship with God

Scarlett

Scarlett believes that a relationship with God as Father is paramount and that God, by his very nature, seeks relationship with others. She holds that getting to know God personally and more deeply is an ongoing journey. As a child, Scarlett never had reason to question what she had been taught about God from Scripture at church but decided to make a public stand for Christ as a teenager. She began to desire a deeper relationship with God through recognizing the presence of the Holy Spirit in others, and at sixteen, she was filled with the Holy Spirit.

Scarlett progressively learned to exercise faith in God and trust him through life's experiences. This resulted in an even deeper understanding of God. However, Scarlett struggled with the notion of trusting God as a father that does good, as it was her father that had abused her. While she knew Jesus as her savior, friend, Lord, and brother, and the Holy Spirit as "an abiding friend" who leads and guides, the whole concept of God as Father was really difficult. For Scarlett learning to trust God as Father was more difficult, and a slower process, than learning to hear the voice of the Spirit. It was through the Holy Spirit showing her God's heart and how he grieves that brought an increased trust that her heavenly Father was working for her benefit. It was experiencing God, his love, and the value he placed on her that built trust and deepened the relationship.

Faith and Calling

Liam

Liam's upbringing included a knowledge of God. He grew up as part of a devoutly Catholic family. He came to Christ at seven years of age. He feels his relationship with God has always been a strong one. It was while serving at church as an altar boy that he received a call to ministry. Being involved in Christian ministry became a priority from very early on. His family transitioned from Catholicism to Pentecostalism while he was still young. He was "baptized in the Spirit" as a teenager. His Christian faith and knowledge kept growing through his teens. He became involved in Christian ministry in a public capacity from very early on. He was involved in youth ministry as a teen and had an ongoing desire to be involved in church ministry.

Summary

These idiographic representations of the world as the context for the activity of the Holy Spirit have disclosed a number of meta-themes in the experience of spiritual healing. The first meta-theme is the world of perceptual phenomena; the second is the "self" and "the other" in relation; and the third is transcendence and immanence.

The Lived World of Perceptual Phenomena

The world is the whole in which we live as historical creatures. It is the context or horizon of all things given to the self as the agent of the natural attitude. By *natural* is meant prior to critical reflection. *Lebenswelt* (lifeworld), the world of lived experience, is "the world of immediate experience," the world as "already there," as "pre-given."[1] It is the world of perception which precedes and is the necessary condition for knowledge. The *natural attitude* is our "default perspective," our "spontaneous experience" of things, situations, facts, and other kinds of objects.[2] It is pre-reflective and pre-theoretical. It is "a reflexive or self-given awareness which is, as awareness, unaware of itself."[3] The *world* as such is a background, a horizon for all things that can be "intended" or given to us—"the ultimate setting for ourselves and all the things we experience."[4] It is a *singulare tantum*.[5]

Another singularity, which is paradoxically both within the *world* and the entity to which the *world* is given or manifested, is the *self*, the *ego*, the I. The world as *singulare tantum*, and the *self*, as the center around which this whole is arranged, "are the two singularities between which all other things can be placed."[6]

1. Husserl, *Crisis of European Sciences*, 103–86.
2. Sokolowski, *Introduction to Phenomenology*, 42–43.
3. Van Manen, *Researched Lived Experience*, 35.
4. Sokolowski, *Introduction to Phenomenology*, 45.
5. The world as a *singular tantum* is the singular context, setting, background, or horizon encompassing all the things that can be given to us; and, as such, is the ultimate setting for all the co-participants' experiences.
6. Sokolowski, *Introduction to Phenomenology*, 45.

The two ingredients of actual experiencing are "the actual material of encounter" and "the one who encounters"[7]—the two go together. The one experiencing must co-exist with, and "stand out against," what there is to be experienced.[8] Experience is "repeated encounter with what is there requiring continuity and identity both in what is experienced and in the one who experiences."[9]

A third structural element to the natural attitude is *world belief*.[10] Awareness or any sense of self could never arise apart from an underlying acceptance of the world and the things in it. While belief about things in the world may be modified and corrected over time, this underlying acceptance of the world and the things in it is always there.

The lived world as experienced through everyday immersion in various situations and relations can be thought of as structured around fundamental existential themes such as wellness, health, life, death, being, meaning, otherness, and mystery. Van Manen suggests four existential themes that probably pervade and belong to the lifeworld of every person (although in different modalities): spatiality (lived space), corporality (lived body), temporality (lived time), and relationality (lived human relation).[11]

Our present space affects the way we feel but is largely pre-verbal. We may feel safe and protected or uneasy and insecure. As humans, our lived experience is in and through our bodies. Our physical presence both reveals and conceals things about us in relation to lived experience. Our lived experience of time is not sequential but lived in this "now" moment. A present space-time activity can revive a memory and mood of the past, making it present. As humans, we also live in relation to other human beings. To be human and be in the world means being-with-others.[12] It is in this experience of the other that human beings have searched "for a sense of purpose in life, meaningfulness, grounds for living, as in the religious experience of the absolute Other, God."[13]

---

7. Smith, *Experience of God*, 32.
8. Smith, *Experience of God*, 32.
9. Smith, *Experience of God*, 30.
10. Sokolowski, *Introduction to Phenomenology*, 45.
11. Van Manen, *Researched Lived Experience*, 101–02.
12. Heidegger, *Pathmarks*.
13. Van Manen, *Researched Lived Experience*, 105.

The World as the Context

These categories help us inquire into deeper levels of meaning. While they can be distinguished, they cannot be separated. They each belong to the rich complexity of the many and varied human lifeworlds.

From the participants' accounts, we can identify further levels. There is world as intense religious activity; world as right-performance; world as disempowerment; world as family dysfunction; and world as church life. Within the world as family and the world as church life exists a further plurality. The world as church life involves the participants' varied religious experiences. This is further apparent if we specify further strata within these. There is world as an austere and demanding God; world as disillusionment with Christian formulas (or world as open to new perspectives); world as admiring Jesus; world as a deepening relationship with God; and world as serving God. The world as family life involves world as regular abuse, and world as enforced provider of sex.

Each participant refers to the place of God in their early lifeworlds. For Chloe everything was God-orientated, but she still asked, "What's real?" Julian had a conversion experience but was still asking deep questions and was open to a new language and a new way of seeing it. Scarlett had no doubts, but "the whole concept of God as father was really difficult." Adam "was surrounded by Christianity from day one," and Jesus Christ had always been his hero. Emma wasn't brought up with any Christianity whatsoever. Julian had a strong relationship with God from childhood. Sophia, while always loving Jesus who was looking after her, hated God.

Interpretation occurs whenever we know we have experienced something. The interpretative element, rather than a post-encounter reflection, is "a receptivity" brought to the encounter. The material of the encounter and the one who encounters are necessarily linked. The interpreting self "precedes the encounter," "enters into the encounter," and maybe "reflects upon the encounter."[14] If so, one's conceptual understanding can be distinguished from the original encounter through reflection. The original encounter is richer than the reflective conceptual awareness and contains something that escapes rational explanation. One's thoughts about an encounter may be inadequate reflections of that encounter. Every personal encounter has an element of mystery that escapes comprehension. The participants' significant questioning of early concepts of God, leading to a deepening relationship with God, may attest to their pre-conceptual experiences of God as other. If God is experienced, it is not by sense experience

---

14. Edwards, *Human Experience of God*, 7.

or the grasp of intellect, it is pre-conceptually. Much of our knowing occurs at an implicit level.[15] Polyani refers to "ineffable experiences" as "something that I know and can describe even less precisely than usual, or even only very vaguely."[16]

Both Scripture and theology attest that God is present to us pre-conceptually. The Scriptures are filled with texts that point to the inner experience of God (Rom 5:5; 8:14–16; 8:26). Both Augustine and Aquinas teach that there is a Trinitarian mission to the individual person. Rather than a completely separated God, there is "a constant and permanent divine initiative"[17] toward individuals, who if they are open can be led to a knowledge of God. Smith maintains,

> Revelation or divine disclosure must not be set over against experience as if the latter were *natural* and former *supernatural*. For revelation represents a further development of the experiential matrix of religion, since experience is the only medium through which anything can be revealed to man.[18]

Gregory of Nyssa speaks of approaching God only in darkness, that is, without intellectual comprehension. John of the Cross draws on this long tradition when he uses the image of darkness to express the pre-conceptual experience of God. The symbol, dark night, expresses that while God is accessible to experience, he remains invisible and incomprehensible to human intellect. The symbol emerges out of experience by an inner need to reflect on that experience, even if it is incomprehensible and unspeakable.

The Self and the Other in Relation

The analysis of the participants' transcripts uncovered noematic factors which operate as underlying themes in spiritual healing. The first factor is that we are shaped by our relationships. We are first in a relationship, and then we know ourselves as a center of consciousness apart from those to whom we relate.

The participants' experiences of certain other people and groups of people were influential in their spiritual journey and healing. Chloe was

15. Polyani, *Personal Knowledge*.
16. Polyani, *Personal Knowledge*, 88.
17. Kelsey, *Encounter with God*, 89.
18. Smith, *Experience of God*, 66.

aware of a lack of joy from the people in her church in contrast to the Dalai Lama who seemed "just the jolliest man," indicating her awareness of something missing. Scarlett recalls when a certain lady started coming to her church, she knew, "she's got something, and just whatever it is . . . I wanted it." She now refers to this lady as Spirit-filled. Sophia believed her Christian grandmother "influenced the spiritual dynamics around her." She was touched in a huge way through her early involvement in churches. Emma refers to her Christian grandmother as the one person who really loved her. Julian became good friends with a Christian youth leader who invited him to meetings and eventually he was to make a personal commitment to Christ. Liam was early influenced by itinerant type ministries and initially wanted to be one himself.

Objects-relations theory posits a relational paradigm where, in the preverbal stage of infancy, the self and object world are fused; the dichotomy of self and other do not yet exist. The central self goes through a three-stage process in beginning its formation as separate from the mother: absolute dependence, relative dependence, and toward independence.[19] The needs and gestures of the self find appropriate acknowledgement and engagement of the otherness balanced with a reality that does not conform to its wishes. From early experiences characterized by dialectal splits comes a developing sense of the continuity of objects and of self as integrated mixtures.

It is only with the passage of time and, more importantly, with the mirroring experience provided by the mother in which the infant's need for acknowledgement and confirmation is gratified that the self becomes established. Without this stimulating and confirming experience, the self remains weak and ill-defined. In adult life, people will relate to others and situations as shaped by early infant experiences. While these objects continue to exert strong influences later experiences can reshape the early patterns.

The second noematic factor operating as an underlying theme in spiritual healing is that our relational connections provide a glimpse into the deeper search for self-transcendence. All the participants speak of, or allude to, their experience of certain others giving rise to a perspective of the self-seeking transcendence. It is in the joining of event or experience and interpretative meaning that identity develops through social interaction

---

19. Winnicott, *The Maturation Processes*, 46.

and successfully coping with stage-related dilemmas.[20] This experience provides the basis for the question: Who am I, really?

Human life within the Christian vision can be seen to take place and demand interpretation in three levels of time simultaneously: time within the human life cycle; time within the process of human history; and, time within the structure of the life of God in relation to creation—eschatological time.[21] In the first, there is the compulsion through "human historical embeddedness" to repeat old patterns of self-world interpretation.[22] Sophia conveys that her relatives had been gambling, drinking, and violent for generations. Continually they "regressed back to their hurts and grievances." Life in that context was dim, grey, and black, with no blue on the horizon. Julian indicates, "I'm tired of doing the same old stuff and getting nowhere."

As interpretative answers to the boundary issues of life and death are sought, there is seen the human capacity and desire for self-transcendence. Julian says, "I get to a point in my life and I'm asking some deep questions." Emma says, "Somehow I got hold of the fact that I didn't have to be like that forever."

At the level of historical time, the self's interpretative process is offered a set of socially legitimated interpretative options in which to participate. To the extent that these penetrate to the level of primary object relations, they impinge upon and shape the dynamic forces of the ego. The development of a style of interpretation will be located somewhere between the poles of reification of cultural interpretative modes and the risks of open, unstable interpretations that may lack social support.

Most of the participants speak of coming to realize the abnormality of their lifeworld in relation to the wider social-cultural context. Sophia speaks of the warmth and tranquility she experienced in another home and says, "I thought it was a play put on to impress me." Emma indicates that she didn't allow her friends to come to the family house while also not knowing how abnormal her situation was. Julian talks of the relief in finding that "life till now had never been normal." Each participant reached a boundary in their lifeworld when the wider socio-cultural environment of their historical context penetrated and demanded interpretation or reinterpretation.

---

20. Erikson, *Life Cycle Completed*.
21. Gerkin, *Living Human Document*, 105–17.
22. Moltmann, *Church in the Power*, 192.

The third level of time in the Christian vision within which human individual life and corporate history are contained is time within the purpose and promise of God, eschatological time. In Jesus Christ, a new process was set in motion: the time of God's Kingdom coming into history. Christian life is lived within the *already* of that coming into history of the power of the Kingdom, and the *not yet* of the final fulfillment of that promise and power. When believers participate in that eschatological life and accept their new identity in Christ, there is a change in the self, involving the Holy Spirit. Gerkin asserts that,

> In the gap between the already and the not yet of eschatological time we may by the power of the Spirit experience changes that bring our historical identity into more wholistic balance with our eschatological identity.[23]

All the participants understand their identity to be in Christ and expected change in their lives.

Transcendence and Immanence

This final section is an exploratory discussion of transcendence and immanence in relation to spiritual healing and the activity of the Holy Spirit. The participants' lifeworld experiences include both transcending apprehensions and moments when transcendence breaks into their lives.

Transcending apprehensions are present in the participants' narratives when Chloe was looking for joy; Julian and his wife came to the end of themselves and he says, "That moved us to actually be open to hearing something else"; and Sophia describes her family life as being not from God. In each, there is a felt absence of something to be apprehended.

This transcending pre-apprehension of further possibilities occurs upon an awareness of "being without limits." Rahner demonstrates that whenever our intellects reach out to grasp an individual object they do so only in pre-apprehension which reaches out towards infinite being.[24] Experience of ourselves, of others, and of infinite transcendence always occurs together. All are present within consciousness and dependent upon the other. Whenever an intellectual awareness and grasp of a known person is formed through memory and imagination, there is always a further

23. Gerkin, *Living Human Document*, 157.
24. Rahner, *Spirit in the World*, 142.

obscure awareness of who this person is not. This person is known against a whole range or horizon of being which escapes limits, definitions, and attempts to grasp it intellectually. Rahner says,

> We must . . . ask how the agent intellect is to be understood so that it can know the form as limited, confined, and thus of itself embracing further possibilities. Obviously, this is possible only if, antecedent to and in addition to apprehending the individual form it comprehends of itself the whole field of these possibilities and thus, in the sensibly concretized form, experiences the concreteness as limitation to these possibilities, whereby it knows the form itself as able to be multiplied in this field.[25]

This horizon of being without limits is mystery, a dimension of human experience that escapes comprehension, which totally transcends us, but is at the core of human activity. It is the condition to conceptual knowledge and present all the time in daily life. While always present within the reach of consciousness, though not normally the focus of attention, this horizon of infinite mystery can be attended to. Rahner further points out that,

> If we were simply to say that "God" is the term of our transcendence, then we would have to be continually afraid of the misunderstanding that we were speaking of God in the way that he is already expressed, known and understood beforehand in an objectifying set of concepts.[26]

While we cannot describe for ourselves an infinite being whom we experience, we can say what we experience cannot be limited, and that it moves into infinity. Rahner says,

> Now this *Vorgriff* does not represent the infinite in himself, it only co-affirms him as the ultimate whereunto of the illuminated dynamism of the spirit who we call *Vorgriff*. On the other hand, the *Vorgriff* occurs and we know about it only as the condition of the possibility of conceptual knowledge of finite objects. It seems to follow that we know of God's infinity only in connection with finite beings.[27]

This is one way of attempting to describe how we as human beings come to an awareness of God in our lives. Furthermore, speaking of

---

25. Rahner, *Foundations of Christian Faith*, 61.
26. Rahner, *Foundations of Christian Faith*, 61.
27. Rahner, *Hearer of the Word*, 26.

experience of God is not only consistent with Christian tradition but needful to pastoral care and counseling.

The participants' experiences indicate that, while mystery is an always present dimension of human experience, there are special moments when transcendence breaks in upon one's life in a more obvious way. Sophia never self-harmed or self-destructed as "someone was watching over me" and "there was this peace." Emma refers to a time when "it was like God out of nowhere came into my life and I started to see things differently." Chloe tells how "something happened, and it was like my eyes were opened," and "the first thing God gave me was this amazing vision." Julian senses, "God was really talking to me." Adam says, "God spoke to me about my life and about my ministry." Scarlett also refers to God speaking to her. Julian recalls as a boy he heard a voice call him to Christian ministry.

The participants report something beyond themselves breaking in on their awareness in a mysterious but noticeable way. Edwards has called these experiences of immanent transcendence "moments of grace" because they are experienced as "a gift."[28] These are moments filled with a richness that exceeds our hopes and expectations. The participants have referred to this experience of immanent transcendence as God. In referring to God, the participants are, through experience and interpretation, coming to a conviction about the reality and nature of a unique being in relation to their own meaning and identity.

Here, it is important to distinguish "living reason" from "formal reason." While the latter is "a system of implications between propositions which rest ultimately upon arbitrarily chosen axioms;" the former denotes "the quest on the part of the concrete self for intelligibility."[29] Living reason starts from certain direct experiences and moves toward the discovery of rational pattern and meaning with these experiences. The individual self is fully involved in the movement of thought for the purpose of discovering the rational pattern in its own experience so that a sense of conviction attaches to the conclusion it reaches. For this sense of conviction to be present, the self must participate in the subject matter being analyzed by direct experience. This is in keeping with the Platonic-Augustinian tradition. It is not a question of the existence of God but whether through experience

---

28. Edwards, *Human Experience of God*, 28.
29. Smith, *Experience of God*, 111.

and interpretation one is led to acknowledge "the reality of a unique being possessing that reality in a peculiar way."[30]

Conclusion

In this chapter, I have discussed interpretive themes from the participants' transcripts relating to the world as the place in which God is discovered and encountered. What makes itself apparent as a core theme is that within the consciousness of these victims has been the sense of how both transcending moments, in terms of pre-apprehensions of infinite being and special moments where the beyond, mysteriously and noticeably, breaks into their lived space, make up actual material of their lived world encounters and are interpreted as divine disclosure. I have elucidated the importance of self-transcendence through relationship with others and God as the possibility of identity, meaning, change, and healing finding formation.

---

30. Smith, *Experience of God*, 120.

5

WOUNDEDNESS

Introduction

This chapter addresses the interpretative themes: vulnerability, manipulation and control, internal damage, conflicted inner and outer worlds, images of God, uncovering wounds, rising emotions, and, oversexualization.

Vulnerability, Manipulation, and Control

Liam

Liam found it strange his father moved their conversations from trivia to sex so quickly and so often. This progressed to sexual education activities which were "totally humiliating." The same activities were repeated over and over again by his father. They included comparing the length of sex organs, measuring the duration of an erection, and masturbating. He understood this to be genuine sexual education and a normal part of life. That was reinforced in that the perpetrator was his father and pastor, and that it stopped the day before he got married. His own discomfort and poor performance in these sexual activities left him questioning his own normality.

His father insisted on secrecy by indicating that his mother wouldn't understand. Certain comments he made to his fiancé convinced him she didn't appreciate what was happening and so it was best not to talk about it.

His mother never queried their regular, isolated times together. Even after disclosure, his mother avoided facing the real issue.

His father used flattery to manipulate him into enticing his younger brother into the same sexual activities. He did seek an opportunity to entice his brother but then changed his mind. He was later hurt to think his father actually encouraged him in the abuse of others. He later understood his father to be guilty, fully responsible, and culpable of sexual abuse.

Adam

Adam indicates that in both cases of sexual abuse he didn't understand sexual things. At the time of the first abusive experience, he was completely ignorant of sex. He believed his parents were aware and condoning of what was taking place. He was under the impression with the early abuse that he was being taught. His first perpetrator used sex education as a pretense for his own sexual gratification. His sexual encounter was not necessarily a negative experience at the time. The physical sensation from the early abuse was pleasurable. His first and main perpetrator initiated the abuse by exposing him to pornographic pictures of girls. The sexually abusive experience involved looking at books and then masturbating each other. The initial perpetrator described their sexual experiences as "our secret."

Internal Damage

Scarlett

When the perpetrator justified what he was doing to her, it was difficult for Scarlett to process or respond to. While she ignored his comments, they did impact her deeply. She was left with a sense of self-blame. She also wrongly devalued many things about herself. Inwardly she was very angry. Her low self-esteem dictated both the value she placed on herself and her negative self-talk. All the while, she understood that God placed a higher value on her than she placed on herself. The mistrust she experienced regarding her feelings about herself had, she believes, been intentionally introduced and reinforced. This indoctrination process involved the elevation of her father's views over and above her own. Her own feelings weren't allowed any credibility. In her unhealed state, she wasn't acknowledging and taking notice of her own feelings. She realized later that there was an absence of feelings.

Inner and Outer Worlds

Julian

Julian's sexual abuse gave rise to the use of pornography and masturbation as ways of trying to experience good feelings. These substituted for the previous sexual encounters and continued into adulthood and married life. Engaging in pornography left him deeply angry. He was incensed by the feeling of defeat. His anger was directed at himself and his situation. He was also angry with God for the injustice of being left emotionally vulnerable after the loss of his father. His anger was accompanied by feelings of isolation and aloneness. Feelings of shame and unworthiness became all-consuming.

Julian describes his life as inwardly crying out for help and outwardly doing his best. He compensated for his inner turmoil by trying to get more faith to overcome and being more jealous in Christian ministry. When this produced no inner change, guilt and self-doubt occurred. Beneath this drive to perform was a genuine spiritual desire. He cultivated the ability to be open and truthful to a level that didn't disturb the way that others saw him. He handled conflict and other difficult situations by suppressing his emotions. He would dismiss penetrating questions with superficial responses. He describes his internal reality as "vile black crap" which was just looming and sitting and needing to be released.

Emma

Emma sees she was two persons. One was full of shame and another was fun-loving. Her positive persona was a masquerade to some extent covering over feelings of low self-esteem and of being unusual and rejected. One of her coping mechanisms was to throw herself into her work. Overeating was a way of cultivation good feelings. She constantly strove to get things right and to please others to prove her worth and normality. Some things were done just to earn the approval of others. Emma also struggled with the idea that she may have been responsible for the abuse as she never stopped it happening. She understands now there is a distinction in the way a child and adult mind interprets the abuse, and that the perpetrator alone is guilty of the abuse.

Images of God

Sophia

There was never a time that Sophia doubted Jesus' caring presence with and for her. She understood God in the way she saw Jesus. He presented a desirable contrast to her background. She was not angry at God as she clearly understood Jesus to disapprove of her abuse. In spite of loving Jesus, Sophia hated the sovereign God and struggled with the concept of God as Father. Her understanding of God the Father was of a human person who used their power to take advantage at the expense of the victim. She only considered the notion of God as Father because Jesus referred to him that way. Her image of God as Father was connected to someone who is all-powerful and requires people to function in ways beyond their capacity.

Emma

While Emma appreciated Jesus as a friend who demonstrated his love through his sacrifice for her, the idea of God as Father was extremely difficult. She didn't feel she could trust him. The idea that God was her father and that he loved her was contradictory. She could not assimilate the notions of "good" and "father" together into any kind of picture. Emma also was not able to trust people in dependent situations. She especially did not trust men. She understood her acute anxiety was due to a complete lack of trust of those in control. She further came to understand that the reason for her anxiety was ultimately her lack of trust in God. God's inactivity in preventing her abuse was felt to be the failure of another male.

Uncovering Wounds

Scarlett

Scarlett describes the internal damage from her abuse in terms of bandaged up infected wounds. It was a very difficult process having to come to terms with the truth and details of the abuse. Getting married and entering into a sexual relationship was a catalyst to understanding that the impact of the abuse was far greater than previously anticipated. It exposed that the experience of intimacy had become intertwined with sexual abuse. Her initial experiences of "freezing up" at counseling sessions lessened as she, in response to the leading of the Spirit, disclosed and exposed those areas where there was "a needed cleansing of infected wounds."

Chloe

As praise had been used to facilitate Chloe's abuse, even genuine and appropriate expressions engendered some level of trauma. Compliments led to introversion, distrust, and trauma. The foremost problem was her lack of self-esteem. Physical intimacy was almost unbearable and re-traumatizing. She did not understand that present sexual experiences were triggering past negative feelings. Chloe blamed herself for not enjoying sexual intimacy. She was confused by the contradiction between the pain of her experience and her understanding of sex as a gift. Chloe had learned to use her outgoing personality to mask her lack of confidence. She believes that for victims, external appearances and beautifiers can mask the wounds and pain within. Functioning in a public capacity in Christian ministry can mask wounds. Chloe believes that disclosure of one's abuse publicly among females in a safe environment is likely to reveal a high number of similar cases.

Rising Emotions

Liam

Liam's discovery that his sexual experiences were not education, but abuse, brought a sense of relief, but then a lot of other feelings had to be adjusted to. There was a deep mistrust of his father. There was some self-pity. There were feelings of shame, embarrassment, and abnormality. Anger was the strongest feeling to repeatedly surface. Liam was unfamiliar with anger as an emotion because it had been repressed. It arose as an eruption of internal rage. It was the strongest emotion he had ever experienced. It was primarily directed at his father for deceiving and manipulating him into things that were wrong. His wife witnessed a personality change in him. He became very aggressive verbally toward his father. He would more easily get irritated, agitated, flustered and frustrated, and quickly and aggressively verbalize what he felt and thought at home. He was now processing his emotions externally. Liam had to learn that anger is a normal part of life. Like other emotions, anger is manageable and doesn't have to dominate.

Oversexualization

Adam

Adam indicates that his early abuse resulted in a distorted way of perceiving sexual matters. It sexualized things in his thinking that would not ordinarily be thought to be sexual. It caused him to have an oversexualized view of people. He indicates that sexual abuse for a male cause them to look at women in a sexual way. Childhood sexual abuse distorts one's thinking, behavior, and outlook regarding sexuality. He believes it is the norm for victims of childhood sexual abuse to suffer from sexual distortions. They have oversexualized perceptions of the world.[1] He understands that seeing people primarily in sexual ways means being blinded to the whole person. He believes this is supported not only from his own life but the experience of other victims. While for Adam this propensity was addressed through spiritual experiences and disciplines, it could be temporarily undone when, suddenly, something goes wrong. He understands consistency in daily prayer is one antidote to the old, oversexualized thought patterns.

Summary

These idiographic representations of the interpretive themes identified in the participants' transcripts have made explicit a number of underlying categories of meaning present to traumatic wounds from experiences of suffering.

In the following section, I will address nomothetically these deeper categories of meaning, addressing the ways in which spiritual meaning can begin to emerge for believers wounded by childhood sexual abuse. The victims' journeys entail facing complex and profound issues raised by suffering and trauma and finding a spiritual path to recovery. I will do this by discussing below three meta-themes: self as myth-maker, self and

---

1. These thought patterns give rise to being overly observant and intrigued by the possibility of catching sight of some ordinarily covered part of the body or undergarments.

world discovered through experience, and human beings as existentially vulnerable.

Self as Myth-Maker

The explications of the participants' transcripts above reveal the human self as an entity in the process of becoming through a dialogical relationship with its whole phenomenal field, including both its-self and its-lifeworld.

Hiltner understands the self as a differentiated portion of the phenomenal field. The phenomenal field is the totality of experience and the total environment is the organism.[2] Human existence is interconnected and deeply intertwined with its environment. Every individual exists in a continually changing world of experience of which he or she is the center. As a result of interaction with the environment, and particularly as a result of evaluational interactions with others, the structure of self is formed.

Some writers find it necessary to distinguish "self" from "person," or "self" and "Self." Atwood and Stolorow distinguished the two by "the concept of the person as an experiencing subject" and "the concept of the self as a psychological structure."[3] At one level, the self represents "the essence of one's personhood and is a source of agency as a person initiates activity in the world."[4] Merton describes this self as indestructible, rooted in God, and always open to discovery, growth, and transformation.[5] It is "holistic, indivisible and timeless."[6] Jung sees self as a treasure hidden in a field, a potential source of richness, containing that which will make us whole, and that is unavailable to us as long as it is buried. It is the ground out of which any separate sense of "self," or feelings of "I," emerge. Winnicott described this "central self" as,

> The inherited potential which is experiencing a continuity of being, and acquiring in its own way and at its own speed a personal psychic reality and a personal body structure.[7]

---

2. Hiltner, *Self-Understanding*, 171.
3. Atwood and Stolorow, *Structures of Subjectivity*, 34.
4. Means, *Trauma & Evil*, 52.
5. Merton, *The Inner Experience*, 7.
6. Grant, *Way of the Wound*, 42.
7. Winnicott, *Maturation Processes*, 46.

At another level, that which has been variously referred to as "self," self-concept, self-image, identity, self-understanding, self-identification, self-organization, personality, "false self," or ego is the conscious, rational "self" which operates according to the dictates of causal and linear thinking. It looks for single explanations and adopts single perspectives on complex phenomena. It constructs a *mythic* understanding of itself and the world for the sake of consistency, coherence, and control.[8] It fears its finiteness and so wants to do without faith, risk, paradox, and ambiguity. As such, it misunderstands and misrepresents its-self and its-world. Hence human beings live with partial versions of self and world.

Humans downsize life in an attempt to protect themselves. Manageable versions of life are forever being concocted. Self and world understandings are forever tentative and therefore never final. May considers humans to be "myth makers" who need to "make sense of a senseless world."[9] Grant maintains that "myths have the potential to organize and give meaning to life-problems dealing with struggle, pain and transformation."[10] Gerkin derives a psychological correlation to the hermeneutical image of the life of the self, taken from Boisen.[11] The life of the self forms an interpretation, a narrative story, whose central task is to hold in coherence and continuity the relationships of the self within itself and with the object world beyond. Gerkin calls this work of the self's life the hermeneutics of the self, or "the life of the soul."[12]

For several participants, making sense of their sexual abuse experiences gave rise to the myth of *sexual experiences between an adult and a child as sexual education*. Several of the participants understood their early sexual experiences to be genuine sexual instruction. For Liam, this mythic understanding persisted into adulthood. His abuse was described as sex education by the perpetrator, who was his father and pastor, thus supporting the assumption that it was normal. This was reinforced by his mother's non-involvement and the termination of the experiences after his marriage. When Liam's fiancé reacted strangely when he mentioned something about

---

8. *Mythic understanding* refers to a person's ability to make sense of a topic using *tools for thinking* that are developed primarily through their exposure to oral language in particular cultural contexts.

9. May, *Cry for Myth*, 15.

10. Grant, *Way of the Wound*, 4.

11. Boisen, *Exploration of the Inner World*.

12. Gerkin, *Living Human Document*, 97–117.

it, he assumed she wouldn't understand and so said nothing. Adam naively thought his parents knew what was being done to him. The notion of sexual instruction was reinforced by being shown pictures of naked girls, questions and answers, and attempts "to show me how your body would work." Adam laments, "I didn't know."

An adjunct to this myth is the idea that *sexual experiences between an adult and a child are harmless*. Adam understands the experiences could superficially be seen as "almost nothings," but the fact is "the things that they were . . . turned me inside out." While Scarlett realized her father's treatment of her resulted in her negative self-talk and a lack of dignity, she didn't think that damage had been done through the sexual abuse. Once married, she found out that there was a lot more damage than she ever imagined. Chloe's abuse was described to her as "his [the perpetrator's] special love" for her. This was reinforced by him being her uncle and an elder in her church. Chloe didn't realize she had been sexually abused for most of her life.

There is furthermore the myth of *family, friends, and church as the comfort and reassurance of safety*. In talking about his abuse, Liam says, "the person was my father and also the pastor of our church." The abuse occurred down in a shed which was attached to the house. Julian was sexually abused by his older cousin. Adam's early abuse took place while his family were staying with friends, and his parents were in the house. In relation to his later abuse, Adam said, "I didn't know that priests abused boys." Scarlett's abuse was by her father who was the one who takes her family to church. Emma's abuse was by her father in the house, and often with her mother in the other room. Sophia was abused by a relative at extended family gatherings in the family home. Chloe was abused by her uncle in his family home. He was also an elder in her church.

When people who were intended to nurture and protect, such as parents, relatives, priests, and pastors, instead violate, a traumatic event has occurred which affects the victim in many ways.[13] Children depend on adults to learn the name of things. Not only do adults help children name tangible things, but intangible things such as good, bad, right, wrong, and love. Children need to be able to trust adults to name things correctly. When children hear messages, such as "this is sexual education," or "this is special love," they often have no way of knowing they are not true. Children

---

13. Langberg, *On the Threshold*, 53. The word *trauma* comes from the Greek word for wound.

depend upon adults to teach them about their own identities and how to relate to others. When a dependent and vulnerable child's body is used for sex, they are left with the impression, and often told, that the shame and guilt are entirely theirs. They are left with partial, and often distorted understandings, of themselves, others, and God.

The victims' personal identity or sense of self is changed by the abuse suffered.[14] While some participants have no recollection of a time that felt normal, several recall a time before the onset of the abuse when the "self" was experienced differently. Chloe found it weird that in the first minute of entering the family home of a childhood friend as an adult, she felt safe and at home. When Julian says, "I know I'm supposed to be just a boy," he's recalling a prior sense of self. Sophia refers to an "inner child" that was abused.

For some, there was the grief over the loss of self that was experienced as real prior to the onset of the abuse. While Julian felt unworthy, dirty, and ashamed, he also felt "I don't deserve this." Emma believes victims have lost their identity. She was both "that child that was shamed . . . broken . . . robbed" and feeling like "the scum of the earth," and the party-goer who pretended. Victims, she says, pretend to be normal and can act normal, but do not feel normal. If told they are loved, they "without a doubt . . . do not believe you." Hart and Montaldo refer to *a self* that the victim loathes, and which often hates to be loved.[15] Scarlett says of the perpetrator, "He taught me, trained me, not to believe my own feelings about myself." Being female had to do with sexual-gratification and so other qualities were dismissed. Self-image and value were tied to sexual usefulness. Scarlett, Emma, and Chloe each felt self-blame as females.

These deep wounds afflicted by sexual abuse threaten to destroy the victim's sense of safety and trust.[16] If the abuse was repetitive, any illusion of security or hope of safety is shattered.[17] Scarlett later suffered panic attacks. When in an elevator alone with another male she said, "Everything within me was screaming out to run, to get away, because it wasn't safe." Emma describes being nearly sick thinking about getting onto a plane in two months' time. When the pilot walked down the aisle she screamed at

---

14. Langberg, *On the Threshold*, 54.
15. Hart and Montaldo, *The Intimate Merton*.
16. Langberg, *On the Threshold*, 55.
17. Langberg, *On the Threshold*, 55.

him, "Why aren't you flying the plane?" The world and people are no longer secure.

Intentional trauma implicates humanity and therefore challenges a victim's capacity and willingness to connect and trust in relationships. The victims' potential to be fully human has been diminished. While Emma pretended to trust, deep down she didn't have trust and didn't trust anyone. If one person can abuse, then all others become potential abusers. Julian said, "There's nowhere . . . safe . . . I can't trust anyone." Even in the marriage relationship, Scarlett couldn't help attributing sexual meanings to every expression of intimacy. The victims' capacity to comprehend was overflowed and the rational need for control had to give rise to a new myth or version of the truth, comprising *the world as unsafe*.

In order to maintain confluence with others, or survive, many forget, repress, or distort original events and maintain the damaged versions of self. These "stalled and stale images of . . . self"[18] become outdated and must be banished when the distortion is exposed through further scrutiny, or memories of events re-surface.[19] At this point, the narrative story "floats between present and past times" as the victim grapples to find the truth.[20] When Liam discovered his sexual experiences were abuse, there was a sense of relief but the sense of mistrust, shame, abnormality, and anger had to be adjusted to. Scarlett realized she'd been believing her father's words about herself, rather than her own intuition, when a single statement caused her to suddenly remember and realize what he had been doing. Chloe had forgotten the abuse until, in a three-day experience in the Holy Spirit, it played back like a movie. She vividly recalled sights, sounds, and smells and realized, she'd been fed a lie and she'd believed the lie.

The pain and solitude experienced by victims have been expressed by Park with the Eastern word *han*.[21] *Han* is the pain of the "sinned-against." It is "the hopelessness and helplessness of the powerless . . . [and] the silence of the wounded."[22] While sinners can repent of their sin, victims cannot repent of their *han*. *Han* needs to be healed. It is "the void of the soul that cannot be filled with any superficial patch."[23] This void is "the abysmal

---

18. Au and Cannon, *Urgings of the Heart*, 9.
19. Grant, *Way of the Wound*, 13.
20. See Goldblatt, "Stories of Longing and Remembrance," 37–41.
21. Park, "The Bible and Han."
22. Park, "The Bible and Han," 14.
23. Park, "The Bible and Han," 47.

darkness of wounded human beings."²⁴ For Sophia, even the language in church services resulted in further wounding. She likens her outlook "to being in a black hole and . . . seeing no way out."

Self and World Discovered in Experience

The explications of the participants' transcripts indicate that their encounters with the world and the persons in it transcend their subjective understandings.

Rational consciousness is not the primary way that human beings know reality. Polanyi argued that human knowing does not start with either theory or practice but is a constant dialogue between conceptual frameworks that interpret experience and the evidence that has to be accounted for. Human beings encounter, or come up against, something with a depth or dimensions of meaning, yet to be penetrated.

Encounter, as the beginning of experience, involves the one who experiences and "the what" of the experience. Smith maintains that "experience is at the very least a dyadic affair and it is even possible that it be triadic in character, but it is certainly not monadic in the sense of being bare, sensible content."²⁵ The encounter is the surface in need of further penetration in order to face the object. In the most basic sense,

> Experience is the many-sided product of complex encounters between what there is and a being capable of undergoing, enduring, taking note of, responding to, and expressing it.²⁶

Experience involves beings capable of having the encounter, apprehending it, feeling itself in the encounter, and capable of interpreting and expressing the results.

The gaps between encountering, interpreting, and expressing take time. Every "thing" encountered has a depth beyond the surface which can only be penetrated by various interactions, whether physically or intellectually, between the self and what is encountered. These interactions give rise to differing views of the thing encountered and how it is to be interpreted.

The self is discovered and formed through this ongoing reflective process. The world presented to the self is so rich and complex in content and

---

24. Park, "The Bible and Han," 47.
25. Smith, *Experience of God*, 36.
26. Smith, *Experience of God*, 33.

meaning, it cannot be adequately and completely described as a record of what is actually there or viewed by immediate insight without reconsideration. Scarlett intuitively challenged her father's statement, "Women never mean no," but found the meaning too hard. Years later, in a moment of insight, the event was recalled, and the meaning interpreted.[27] This enabled her to express the facts of the experience with new and truer meaning both in regard to herself and the intent of her father's words. Scarlett's experience of fatherhood further made "the whole concept of God as father . . . really difficult." She thought, "How can I trust God to make decisions that are good for me and not just good for him?" This was resolved in a God-encounter which was interpreted as God enjoying spending time with her.

The participants refer to feeling themselves in the abusive encounter in ways that precede interpretation. At the time of the abuse, all Liam could say was that he "hated sex education in the family," and that he felt uncomfortable, abnormal, and ashamed. Chloe didn't consciously know that what was happening to her was wrong, nonetheless for years she "couldn't bear the smell of sperm" without being made to "feel like vomiting." Julian says, "I can't even put my finger on what the emotion is in that experience. In a sense, it was pretty numbing. At the same time there was this incredible feeling that . . . there is something not quite right with this; you know I felt quite dirty in it."

In these experiences, reality confronts with an insistence of its own and places the experiencer under a demand to reflect in a way that does full justice to the nature and being of what is encountered. The experiencing person belongs to reality not simply as a theoretical knower, but as

> One who lives in and through experience, who puts questions both to the world and to himself, and who has an interest in experience as the source of life and understanding.[28]

Experience will not be restricted to a theoretical knowledge which reveals no more than what current language can express. Julian says, "I get to a point in my life and I'm asking some deep questions and I'm open to a new language—I'm open to a new way of seeing it because I'm just tired of doing the same old stuff and getting nowhere." Sophia says she now has words for what was, at the time, "just a black hole inside."

---

27. Patton says that Boisen found in the persons he studied a belief in *the revelatory power of experience*.

28. Smith, *Experience of God*, 25.

From the discovery of the self, there is the knowledge of the possibility of error. Desires and expectations project an intentional and pre-reflective net around possibilities trying to emerge in any given situation. These pre-reflective attunements to reality greatly affect what meanings will be selected and experienced in the phenomenal present.

Most people have a strong desire to maintain current understandings of self. Their wish is to design a once-and-for-all version of self and prevent the incessant flow of becoming. Survivors' egos will resist relinquishing their hold on consciousness through avoidance and superficial band-aiding. It is, therefore, necessary for survivors to learn to take responsibility for how they contribute to the meanings they encounter in any given situation.

Failure to make oneself available to new meanings has wide-reaching consequences. Attempts to create fixed and inflexible versions of self and reality are disruptive and destructive to the further dialogue with one's true self and others needed for healing to be possible. The psycho-spiritual demands of survivors' wounds will not be silenced until such dialogue begins. As Julian said, "You put up a front but, in a sense, you are sought of screaming out."

Experience is the result of an ongoing process involving cooperation. Ongoing life and new social experience expose one to new experiences which may challenge one's present self-understanding. The conflicts that develop need to be addressed. Repeated encounters, over time, together with the critical comparisons of results with other distinct selves, are necessary before something is revealed fully and completely. The errors and illusions that arise within experience can be detected and possibly eliminated by distinguishing between what is merely idiosyncratic and what is inter-subjective.

Human Beings as Existentially Vulnerable

Forgetting that one is a limited being without ultimate answers influences many to become selves of their own making, and recoil against that which is beyond conscious control. The taken for granted is usually not examined until it breaks down.[29] The trauma of suffering, especially useless, senseless suffering, can destroy self-understanding, reveal the ground of uncertainty

---

29. Heidegger, *Being and Time*.

and complexity lying beneath the ego, and undermine abilities to cope and feel safe in the world.[30] Long says,

> In the experience of suffering persons come up against the limits of what can be accounted for in ordinary terms and point towards transcendent reality . . . Suffering may bring us up against our finiteness and may clear our being in the world of the gods of self-deification.[31]

When the ego is displaced, its tendency to circumscribe that which is beyond its power is exposed. The trauma of suffering has the power to take rational consciousness beyond its limit and fling it into mystery and transcendence. It unquestioningly demonstrates that survivors are vulnerable and incapable of protecting themselves. With the collapse of the taken for granted, and without the ordinary perspective of ego-consciousness, a world of disturbing and unlimited possibilities is opened which threatens the survivors' engulfment by non-being and nothingness.

The trauma of childhood sexual abuse can reveal not only the survivors' personal and social vulnerabilities but also existential vulnerabilities. Physical, rather than theoretical, encounters with evil and personal limitations throw structures that are designed to protect into question. They have been exposed to the callous and cruel side of humanity.

When Scarlett realized the deliberate nature of what her father had done, it meant facing who he really was. Liam recalls the shock of realizing his father had tried to "push . . . [him] into doing the same sort of thing" with his brothers. Emma talks of how her experiences cause her to get "horrendously upset with cruelty" and not understand it. When she asks how is it that a father can do that to a child, she is asking how and why this does exist. This kind of senseless suffering in contradicting any human value or purpose eludes integration into any rational or coherent order. Emma also remembers that she used the abuse to make the perpetrator buy her things. She asks, "What made me do that?" And she describes what she did as bad and evil. In linking her evil with that of the perpetrator's, she is hinting at a potential that is universal.

Myths, or surface level understandings, such as *the world as safe*, *myself in control*, and *God as predictable* are inadequate. The inadequacy evokes a sense of the precariousness of existence and points to the desire for

---

30. Levinas, "Useless Suffering," 371–80.
31. Long, "Suffering and Transcendence," 139.

self-transcendence which is at the source of everything that is specifically human. The destruction of self-understanding exposes the foundation of all human identities and the human condition as structured with ambiguities. There is the tension between the human need for the joy and satisfaction of loving and being loved, and the ruptures of death, disappointment, and loss. Nelson, with insights from Kierkegaard, Niebuhr, and Farley says,

> Life is so structured that it presents human creatures in our finitude and freedom with a condition of anxiety that begs for resolution. It pulls and tears at human beings, on the one hand threatening our sense of well-being and survival, while on the other throwing us off-center by the weight of its freedom and possibility.[32]

Humans are ontologically insecure, being haunted by incompleteness, uncertainty, and restlessness at the core of their being. While "yearning to know," there is "the fear of not finding answers," "the fear of facing the abyss," or "knowing what we do not know."[33] This is a void in need of solace and assurance which the human mind, by a mere set of beliefs available through religion, theology, psychology, anthropology, science, and philosophy, cannot provide. Even the orthodox theology of Job's three friends provides no way out of "the agony of the bottomless pit that any human being could hardly bear."[34]

A central theme in the contemplative Christian tradition is that "knowing God is much more like *unknowing* than it is like possessing rationally acceptable beliefs."[35] Survivors are forced to acknowledge their limitations and impoverishments. Merton describes this as the deep, confused, and metaphysical awareness of a basic antagonism between self and God which is due to an estrangement from him by a perverse attachment to self which is illusionary.[36]

While "the loss of self" can lead to impaired ways of being in the world, it can also lead to the encounter of the ego to the Self, the dialogue between the conscious and the unconscious, which Jung held led to *the transcendent function*. Lamborn says,

32. Nelson, "For Shame, For Shame," 73.
33. Moore, "Teaching Justice and Reconciliation," 146.
34. Park, "The Bible and Han," 50.
35. Bachelard, "Foolishness to the Greeks," 105. Both the contemplative Christian tradition and pastoral theology assert the difference, strangeness and hiddenness of God as well as asserting his similarity and closeness to human beings.
36. Pembroke, *Moving Toward Spiritual Maturity*, 105.

Through our encounters with the Self, we are offered a route of connection with that which moves us beyond our limited ego-perspectives—even beyond the psyche itself. It is this *something beyond*, this generative illuminating Presence, which is referenced by such notions as *the infinite* or God. Though the transcendent function cannot be equated with the Transcendent. I think we can gain a glimpse of the Transcendent through its mediation. We might even go on to forge a vital relationship with this Transcendence and find ourselves living from a new Center.[37]

Lamborn further says,

> To be religious is to be receptive to the transcendent source of being, to consent to its functioning within—not just outside of us, as something external and beyond, but inside . . . right at the center of our lives.[38]

The participants' journeys indicate that acknowledging their vulnerabilities within the context of the Christian myth connected them to the possibility of something greater than themselves providing them with the opportunity for transformation.[39] Au and Cannon say spiritual transformation involves two movements: self-appropriation and self-transcendence.[40] Self-appropriation "requires a habit of self-reflection that attunes us to the currents and under-currents of our lives."[41] Self-transcendence refers to "the gradual transformation of . . . ego-centered vision and choices."[42] Conn says,

> Self-transcendence occurs in our effective response to the radical desire of the human spirit for meaning, truth, value and love—a radical desire that is, at bottom, always a desire for God.[43]

Reaching the limit of that which can be done rationally and letting go of the expectation that life can be controlled has been described as "trusting

---

37. Lamborn, "Who Will Stir the Water for Us?," 173.
38. Lamborn, "Who Will Stir the Water for Us?," 173.
39. Not all myths are of equal value. The Christian myth is realistic and concrete; its roots are in actual history, in events that really happened.
40. Au and Cannon, *Urgings of the Heart*, 3.
41. Au and Cannon, *Urgings of the Heart*, 3.
42. Au and Cannon, *Urgings of the Heart*, 3.
43. Conn, "Self-Transcendence," 324.

life's creating power."[44] Human life is best lived as open to the power of the future. Such a life requires a continuous process of transformation as old human structures of meaning are carried over and transformed by the in-breaking power of the open-ended future. Grant holds this is to be the ground out of which any authentic relationship with the Spirit can emerge, and that deeper dialogues with Self and Spirit are needed before authentic transformation and peace can be experienced.[45]

Conclusion

For the wounded human soul struggling to make its way through inward complexity, pain, and profound life issues related to the trauma of childhood sexual abuse, there is little to which it can turn except its own inward counsel in an attempt to make sense of its experiences and protect itself. The hopelessness and helplessness of the powerless victim leaves a void in the soul which cannot be healed with a superficial patch. Forced to acknowledge their vulnerabilities, limitations, and impoverishments, victims are left with the need for something greater than themselves to provide the opportunity for authentic transformation and peace. Issues of ultimate concern are raised which cannot be addressed by a mere set of beliefs.

---

44. Ashbrook, *Minding the Soul*, 20.
45. Grant, *Way of the Wound*.

6

FAITH COMMUNITY

Introduction

THIS CHAPTER ADDRESSES THE place of the Christian community in the believer's experience of and relationship with God including: coming to personal faith in Christ and becoming part of the Christian community; the communal nature of life and spiritual development; and "the horizon of hope" opened up through Christ, reflected and proclaimed, however imperfectly, in and through the church. As Moltmann says, "the church sees itself in the presence of the Holy Spirit as the messianic people destined for the kingdom of God."[1]

The interpretative themes dealt with in this chapter are spiritual foundations, encouraging influences, personal and spiritual growth, cultivating the spiritual life, community and identity, mixed church experiences, counseling and prayer, and ministerial life and experience.

Spiritual Foundations

Sophia

Sophia considers it a blessing that she was introduced to Jesus as a child. She wonders whether never self-harming may be due to knowing Jesus

---

1. Moltmann, *Spirit of Life*, 289.

from an early age. Her involvement in evening church contributed significantly to keeping her on the right track as a teenager. Later she recognized how tremendously she had benefited from various forms of Christian input and contact. Her early faith fortified her from what would have been worse outcomes. She links her disallowing the sexual abuse to progress to intercourse to having been recently confirmed. She attributes her stability as a teenager to her church involvement providing her with a foundation and certainty in life.

Emma

Emma's early knowledge of God enabled her to realize she didn't have to be shaped by her family's image of her. She believes her knowledge of God preserved her from a destructive lifestyle. She was never mentally ill, depressed, promiscuous, or having sexual problems later in marriage because of her abuse. Therefore, her healing journey involved healing from the damage incurred through the abuse alone and not from her own actions. This hastened the healing process. Even when recovery was difficult, her conviction was that God's purpose was to bring her into a better life.

Encouraging Influences

Sophia

When Sophia reflects on her early love for Jesus, she recognizes her grandmother's influence on her. As a child, she began to see the discrepancy between what she saw in Scripture and her home life. The people who profoundly affected her had a disposition and behavior that radically contrasted to her family experience. They responded well even in difficult circumstances and were sincere, truthful and consistent in their responses. This made them highly attractive. The tranquility and godliness she experienced in a Christian family home pervaded the atmosphere in a tangible way. These people impacted her as safe. They indicated "another way to live."

Personal and Spiritual Growth

Scarlett

Scarlett holds that the faith she had grown up with was confirmed in her daily experience, which resulted in the conviction that it was a faith that was true. As she learned to walk by personal faith in God, she experienced spiritual growth. Getting water baptized was a significant step forward, spiritually, which resulted in a greater ability to assert herself. The counseling process that Scarlett entered into resulted in an awareness of self-advancement and a sense of increased internal strength. Part of the growth process involved confession and bringing things to light which resulted in bondages being broken and further freedom. Growing spiritually was necessary for healing. It enabled her to integrate the benefits of the counseling process into her character and life.

Cultivating the Spiritual Life

Sophia

Sophia holds that victims of childhood sexual abuse have been spiritually affected and so healing involves the revival of spiritual life. Secular counseling and natural effort are of no avail in spiritual healing. Sophia believes, in receiving Christ, the inner candle of the spirit was lit. Afterwards, the flame could be increased by regular spiritual encouragement from others. Spiritual encouragement can cultivate an inner spiritual life through sharing the word of God that makes the flame inextinguishable. It can be helped by what others have put into books, tapes, and online, but without personal contact with church, it is more difficult.

Sophia was challenged by God to read Christian literature rather romance novels. Reading books on the Holy Spirit helped her understand how to fan her spiritual flame. This not only kept her growing but also led her to a revelation of God as her Father. She indicates the high value of listening to Christian praise and worship in the healing and growth process. She utilized Christian music as a major source of therapeutic help. She also describes speaking in tongues as not only making her feel really good but as a spiritual force against spiritual powers.

Community and Identity

Emma

Finding and knowing that God called her his child, giving her a new identity and making her part of his family, was of paramount importance to Emma finding healing. She experienced great benefit in understanding that God purposed, valued, and destined her life. That God had created her knowing what her life would hold meant he designed her with his power to defeat her deficiencies. Knowing she belonged to God who loved her and didn't judge her enabled her to continue to come to him and his Word with her struggles and find change take place over time.

Emma is aware of the influence of certain people in the church who helped her adjust her behavior, develop her skills, and assisted in her spiritual and healing journey. She attributes this to the hand of God. Emma was greatly impressed when after disclosing to her pastor, he responded to her no differently. Her personal confidence was helped by a pastor's wife and some other church leaders. She has received spiritually transforming insights from preached messages and Christian songs resulting in change.

Mixed Church Experiences

Sophia

Sophia stopped attending church as a teenager feeling unworthy because of her background. On returning to church, she over-volunteered through a need to please others. She gave people the impression that all was well in her life. However, the discrepancy between her limited capacities through brokenness, and what the church seemed to be asking of her, led to resentment. She had negative experiences with seemingly mature people whom it happens had not been healed themselves. She can understand why abuse victims often do not open up in churches. Even well-intended answers can be unhelpful. Victims can react or be wounded from the scriptures. Cut-and-dry statements in Scripture can be awkward and difficult. Preaching that emphasizes sinfulness rather than God's healing can impact negatively. Sometimes behind sin, there is a deeper problem. Preaching rooted more in pop-psychology than biblical truth is unhelpful to victims as it leaves them in defeat and without the necessary power of the Spirit.

Faith Community

Counseling and Prayer

Liam

Liam appreciated being able to talk things out with a Christian counselor that had been bottled up. However, he felt the counseling was going over the same ground rather than dealing with the real issues. The real change came with prayer counseling where the team invoked the guidance of the Holy Spirit and things were cut off in Jesus' name. They were dependent on God through prayer to reveal what needed to be addressed. Unexpected but relevant things came up for prayer.

This was a time when the Holy Spirit was working to bring release and healing. He was encouraged by the pertinence of the issues prayed about. He began to see that God was working in areas he had been unaware of. He was surprised by the prayer for him to be his own person rather than controlled. He had never perceived it to be the problem until then. Other issues were revisited at a deeper level. He was overcome with emotion when they really hit the nail on the head. The outcome of the prayer ministry sessions was feeling release and that things had been dealt with. God dealt with things when the time was right and other things over time.

Ministerial Life and Experience

Adam

Adam indicates his call to ministry came from a voice from God and not from anyone or anything else. He appreciates how much his rectors and spiritual guides taught him with regard to church ministry. He sees himself as a pastor and cure-of-souls. In one pastorate, he learned that through tragedy God is present. He holds that an abusive background can make you "a savior of people." He wanted to help children from dysfunctional homes with physical and emotional disabilities.

Even after ordination and being actively involved in ministry, Adam was uncertain about the work of the Holy Spirit. Five years in a certain pastorate didn't lead to any personal spiritual growth. He now maintains that the power of the Holy Spirit is either not understood by most believers or is greatly underestimated. Many ordained ministers in traditional churches who have been filled with the Spirit, he believes, have not shared their experience with their congregations through fear. He feels "the awe and worship and majesty" we give to Jesus and the Father is lacking for the Spirit.

Summary

These idiographic representations of the interpretative themes identified in the participants' self-reports have uncovered a number of underlying categories of meaning within the experience of spiritual growth and healing for Christian believers. In the following section, I will discuss nomothetically three sets of interconnected structures or meta-themes. These themes are communion with God involving community with others, community as spiritual and personal formation, and Christian community as openness to God's promised future.

Communion with God Involving Community with Others

All seven participants are actively involved in local churches. Two female and two male recovered victims are ordained ministers, and the others have functioned in teaching and leadership roles. There are several ways the participants came to a personal faith in relation to the Christian church community. These can be divided into three groups.

One group attended church as children and continued to do so as adults. These had experiences leading to a personal faith at different points in their spiritual journeys. Adam, Scarlett, Liam, and Chloe attended church as children with their families and continued to attend as adults. Adam made a public profession as an adult. Scarlett made a public stand as a teen. Liam made a commitment to Christ at seven. Chloe, at a bible college, prayed and something happened, and her eyes were opened. These participants were exposed to the normal channels of instructions, teaching and preaching, from an early age guiding them in how to live, as well as being exposed to structures designed to foster mutual care. Grenz maintains that

> reaching and teaching form the primary means for instilling and maintaining the common commitment to the shared values and mission of the community [and] bringing members of the church together [into various smaller groups] offer[s] opportunities for

fostering meaningful relationship and strengthening bonds of support and accountability.[2]

While each recovered victim in this group has a different and unique spiritual journey, each came to a personal conviction and faith through ongoing participation in church life and community.

A second group experienced God outside the Church and later started attending a local congregation. Sophia's grandmother introduced her to Christ and her foster parents later allowed her to go to a church. Emma made a decision for Christ at fifteen after a brief involvement in church life but says that God came into her life out of nowhere much later. She then started attending a small church. Both attribute significance to their early exposure to Christian teaching within and outside of church.

A third group, of one person, experienced God within a Christian community after being invited to church as an adult. Julian was invited by a good friend to a youth group and later heard a message that resonated. He found himself having to surrender something but not knowing why. This was his first spiritual experience, a faith experience which led to a whole new life and, over time, it led him to become totally absorbed in church life.

While several of the participants' initial experiences of church were casual and superficial, and several participants report experiences involving hurts, disappointments, and conflicts, each nonetheless expressed a need to belong to a community of faith. Adam always loved church. Liam felt it was about the people. Emma had to know that she was born again into a new family. Scarlett, as a child, experienced genuine love at church. Sophia was embraced by families at church. Chloe, Adam, Emma, and Julian have experienced a call to serve in the church as ordained ministers.

This sensed need for belonging and community is consistent with human sciences and also the biblical narratives. Both recognize community as crucial to many aspects of human living. Community is a place of belonging, "a place where people are earthed and find their identity."[3] The very first community to which people belong is the family. Emma referred to the church as her needed "new family." This need for communion is "the most fundamental need of every human-being, the source of all other needs and desires." If that need is not satisfied, "the pain of anguish rises up and with

---

2. Grenz, *Theology for Community*, 646.
3. Vanier, *Community and Growth*, 13.

it feelings of guilt, anger and hate."[4] Merely to be excluded or to sense rejection brings hurt and vulnerability to fear and negativity.

From the narrative of the garden of Genesis to the new earth of Revelation, the drama of the Scriptures speaks of community and indicates that human beings are ontologically social in nature. In the beginning, God said, "Let us make humankind in our image" (Gen 1:26) and then "male and female he created them" (Gen 1:27). As Zizioulas put it "The *nature* of God is communion."[5] The Greek Fathers stressed that,

> [the] three are not individuals but persons, beings whose reality can only be understood in terms of their relations to each other, relations by virtue of which they together constitute the being (ousia) of the one God.[6]

In the creation narrative, the female delivers the male from his isolation. O'Donohue says, "the hunger to belong is at the heart of our nature . . . .the soul hungers for relationship . . . it . . . longs to belong—and it . . . makes all belonging possible."[7]

This "relational self," Grenz argues, is also the "ecclesial self." The *ecclesia*, the church, is believers brought out of isolation into community. A personal response to, and appreciation of, God's saving love leads to a "new sociality" where to be a human person means "to be created in and for God with other human beings . . . [which is] the true form of the human being."[8] This "shared experience"[9] with God and others is what human beings long for and have been, and are being, created for. As Bolsinger puts it,

> *What we really want* is to be accepted just as we really are and to become all we are meant to be. *We want to belong* to a community that welcomes us in all our painful brokenness and helps us to be healed and transformed into more than we ever imagined. *We all want to be loved* and transformed by love.[10]

---

4. Vanier, *Community and Growth*, 14.
5. Zizioulas, *Being as Communion*, 134.
6. Gunton, *Promise of Trinitarian Theology*, 39.
7. O'Donohue, *Eternal Echoes*, xvi, xvii.
8. Chia, "Trinity and Ontology," 459.
9. Grenz, *Created for Community*, 79.
10. Bolsinger, "It Takes a Church," 21. Italics mine.

Faith Community

The church as a community reflecting God's being can, as such, be said to be "a vestige of the Trinity"[11] or indirectly "analogous" to the being of God: "the Church is what it is by virtue of being called to be a temporal echo of the eternal community that God is."[12] This experience of persons-in-community moves the believer out of isolation and into godly relationships with others, *koinonia,* or community. The notion of being in relationship with God as an individual is not only a distortion of Scripture, but

> all the burden of responsibility of the human partner in this relationship comes down on ... God's chosen partner ... [an] ideal ... simply unattainable, even with the help of God's grace.[13]

As "Jesus and the Christian community are one" and "this community is Christ," persons-in-community become "part of the relationship between the Father and the Son."[14] Hence, "basic reality at its heart is community—reciprocal, loving, active community."[15]

Conversion to Christ means an indwelling by the Spirit of Christ for every believer. This indwelling is by none other than "the Spirit of the relationship between the Father and the Son" constituting the body of Christ.[16] Each participant affirmed the reality of this indwelling in their lives.

Community as Spiritual and Personal Formation

For the participants, the community of faith was significant not only in the presentation of the object of faith and in the process of coming to faith, but also in the sustaining and developing of that same Christian faith. They see themselves as gaining a *new identity* in Christ, discovered through, and appropriated within, the context of the community of faith. The faith community embodies, though imperfectly, a way of being and living in the world that is shaped by the Spirit of God, and progressively conforms to the person of Christ. They understand their continuing participation in

---

11. Chia, "Trinity and Ontology," 454.
12. Gunton, *On Being the Church,* 75.
13. Sarot, "Trinity and Church," 37.
14. Sarot, "Trinity and Church," 38.
15. Meek, *Loving to Know,* 361.
16. Grenz, *Created for Community,* 160.

"the fellowship of disciples"[17] to be instrumental in this ongoing spiritual and personal development. All of the participants indicate, directly or indirectly, that their spiritual and personal growth is in the context of *the body of Christ*.

The narrative of a person's life is always embedded in the story of the communities in which the person participates. Lemke says,

> meanings are . . . made . . . by persons . . . within an ecosocial system that minimally includes other persons and the things they make meaning about and that minimally operates over timescales sufficient for a developing person to come to engage in socially meaningful interactions with others and with the nonhuman surround.[18]

Central to the knowing process is the cognitive framework mediated to the individual by the community in which one participates. The community is crucial in the process of identity formation because it mediates the transcending story, within which a person finds a set of categories that brings together the diverse aspects of their own lives into a meaningful whole and enables the construction of their own story. Lemke says personal identity can be called "a semiotic articulation of a person's evaluative stance toward interactions."[19] Personal stories are never isolated units but touched by the stories of other persons and ultimately the communities of which one is a part. To find oneself then, one must find the story in terms of which one's life make sense.

Incorporation into the community of Christ becomes the means whereby a new cognitive framework and a new identity is mediated to the participating individuals. The meta-narrative of the Christian community is the gospel story: God has acted on peoples' behalf through the person and work of Jesus Christ, making provision for a complete salvation from the results of sin. And that Christ's life, death, resurrection, and ascension resulted in God's Spirit being active in the world to make the saving work of Christ efficaciously and personally real, initiating new spiritual life in people, ultimately completing God's saving work from sin so that they may permanently participate in an eternal fellowship with God and others.

This story of God's redemption is transmitted by the believing community from generation to generation, mediating the framework for the

---

17. Grenz, *Created for Community*, 197.
18. Lemke, "Across the Scales of Time," 283.
19. Lemke, "Across the Scales of Time," 283.

FAITH COMMUNITY

formation of personal identity, values, and a worldview. Every saving encounter has involved the faith community, the church of Jesus Christ, through which the proclamation of the gospel has been received. Through the life of the community, those who have not yet come to faith may repeatedly encounter the gospel message in spoken, enacted, and lived proclamation. Grenz puts this into perspective when he says,

> we are confronted with the gospel because the community of Christ's faithful disciples has remembered, preserved and guarded the story of God's activity. And through its representative this believing community . . . has now announced the story to us. Even if we come to faith, simply by reading the Bible, the community is still at work, for the Scriptures contains the one church of Christ announcing the gospel.[20]

In community, Christians become aware of and begin to apply their newfound identity *in* Christ. Contrary to post-modern psychology, which insists we together create our own identity, the participants came to understand that their origin, true identity, and destiny were to be found in God. Through involvement in a church community, the participants began to view, experience, and speak about themselves and the world in light of God's action in Jesus Christ. As Sophia puts it "Some days I get up and still don't like who I am as a person, but boy do I like who I am in Christ." Grenz says,

> In conversion, we reinterpret our personal story in light of the story of the Christian community and the categories it exemplifies. Following the biblical narrative, we speak of "old" and "new," "being lost" but "having been found," "sin" and "grace." Reinterpreting our story in this manner entails accepting the story of the Christian community as our own. We are now a part of *this* people; we are incorporated into *this* community.[21]

The Christian life can be described as the process of *enjoying* who one is *to* Christ and *becoming* who one is *in* Christ.

The church understands itself to be the body of Christ, a covenant community, and the household of God, images involving the basic dynamic

---

20. Grenz, *Created for Community*, 195.
21. Grenz, *Created for Community*, 195.

of *belongingness, responsibility,* and *interrelatedness.*[22] In short, belonging is for becoming. Grenz says,

> Christ calls us to build each other up, so that we might all become spiritually mature (Eph 4:11–13). Mutual edification is crucial to us all. The Christian life is not merely an individual struggle for perfection. Rather, in an important sense, it is a community project.[23]

The church as a community of people sharing a common salvation is crucial in the spiritual and personal growth and development of each member. As Meek puts it, "knowing is . . . not mere information [but] transformation."[24] It is transformative because "its dynamic is interpersonal."[25] Personal relationship transforms epistemically. The community of faith catalyzes transformation because "what transforms us, in our knowing, is not *a what* but *a who*."[26] Salvation is "an all-encompassing process"[27] beginning with conversion and continuing throughout life in the fellowship of the church.

It was while studying at Bible College that Chloe came to personal faith, and experienced God speaking to her. The next day she told the assembled college, "Last night I was born again by the Holy Spirit." Sophia refers to her confirmation as a possible catalyst to being established in Christ and pushing away the darkness in stages. Scarlett refers to water baptism as a huge step forward in her walk with God, resulting in more confidence and boldness. Ongoing involvement with other Christians and a home-group led to a continual journey of learning more. For Julian, coming to Christ meant a new view on life. He became involved in various roles of youth ministry and found himself wanting to help people and share the Gospel with as many people as he could. Having been involved in church all his life, Adam found he felt called to train for the sacred ministry.

Irrespective of the ways the participants came to a personal faith, each responded to God's saving action in Christ through the activities of a believing community. Each participant encountered the gospel, responded, and was incorporated into a believing community, and each participant

---

22. Hiltner, *Theological Dynamics*.
23. Grenz, *Created for Community*, 222.
24. Meek, *Loving to Know*, 131.
25. Meek, *Loving to Know*, 136.
26. Meek, *Loving to Know*, 137.
27. Grenz, *Created for Community*, 198. Italics mine.

began a journey of discipleship, discovering and appropriating their identity in Christ through the community of faith.

Christian Community as Openness to God's Promised Future

The believing community of the church is also the eschatological community witnessing to the triumph of God's kingdom accomplished in Jesus. The Gospels report Jesus preaching and teaching the kingdom, and also claiming that the kingdom of God had come in his person and mission (Matt 12:28). In seeking to expound "how and in what sense" the eschatological kingdom had become "a present reality," Ladd concludes that: God has acted on the plane of history "to bring history to a divinely directed goal"; evil is "a terrible enemy of human well-being" greater than human beings and only overcome by "the mighty intervention of God; God's redemptive activity in history in Jesus is yet to be fully and publicly manifest; and the church not only "witnesses to God's future victory," but is "to display the life of the eschatological kingdom in the present evil age."[28] The "powers of the age to come" are already manifest (Heb 6:5), the "strong man" is already being bound (Matt 12:29; Mark 3:22–27), and victims are already being released (Luke 4:18).

It was through Christ's resurrection that this present evil age is *already* overcome. Moltmann says,

> In Christ's resurrection we recognize the presence of God's promised future, deliverance from evil, and the beginning of the good new life; the overcoming of sin, hell, and death, and the beginning of eternal life; the end of godforsakenness . . . and the beginning of a universal, liberating, and rejoicing indwelling of the living God in all things.[29]

Christian faith presupposes the resurrection of Jesus—it is "the starting point" of Christian hope: "Jesus is not dead; Jesus lives; and we shall live with him in eternity."[30] It was perceived by the disciples as *"the beginning, the beginning of true life, the beginning of God's kingdom, the beginning*

---

28. Ladd, *Presence of the Future*, 331, 333, 337.
29. Moltmann, *Presence of God's Future*, 578.
30. Moltmann, *Presence of God's Future*, 578.

of the new creation of all things."³¹ The early church regarded itself as an eschatological congregation, "the Congregation of the end of days," "the vestibule . . . of God's Reign that [was] shortly to appear."³² While the full presence of the kingdom had not yet come to pass, opposition was doomed to melt away.

The resurrection is the beginning of the transfiguration of history. Hunsinger asserts, "The transcendent mystery of Christ's bodily resurrection, being sui generis, brought history to its categorical limit."³³ *Radical transcendence* and *real historicity* are essential to the uniqueness of the resurrection event. He argues it is not enough to emphasize transcendence or spiritual aspect of the resurrection at the expense of historicity and reduce the resurrection to simply Jesus' "enduring influence" or "spiritual presence,"³⁴ nor is it enough to elevate historicity at the expense of transcendence and reduce it to an actual historical occurrence with only anticipatory realization.³⁵ The continuing spiritual presence and influence of Jesus is not detachable from his resurrection. On the basis of the resurrection, "the whole Christ is present in the Spirit which brings life."³⁶ The early disciples were seized by the power and Spirit of the resurrection.³⁷ While Jesus' death on the cross was a historical fact, his resurrection was an event of a different order; it was "an eschatological happening."³⁸ More than a historical fact, the resurrection is a

> *historical event* that has a confronting impact on the present, opening up the eschatological history of eternal life in the midst of this world of death and inviting every human being to this divine future.³⁹

The Church now thinks and acts eschatologically because it is bound to Jesus by the Holy Spirit.

31. Moltmann, *Presence of God's Future*, 578.
32. Bultmann, *Theology of New Testament*, 37.
33. Hunsinger, *Daybreak of New Creation*, 165.
34. Schleiremacher, *Christian Faith*, 467; Bultmann, "New Testament and Theology," 42; and Tillich, *Systematic Theology*, 157.
35. Pannenberg, *Jesus*, 98; and Wright, *Resurrection of the Son*, 710.
36. Moltmann, *Presence of God's Future*, 581.
37. John 20:22. After the resurrection Jesus breathed on them and said, "Receive the Holy Spirit."
38. Moltmann, *The Way of Jesus Christ*, 214.
39. Moltmann, "Blessing of Hope," 152.

Faith Community

As Moltmann says,

> Since the resurrection of Christ, God's creative Spirit is also the Spirit of Christ, and the Spirit of Christ is also *the power of the resurrection* and of eternal life.[40]

And now,

> the living energies of the Holy Spirit (charismata) are sent by the risen, living and present Christ into the community of his people and into the world. They are the living energies of the future world (Heb 6:5).[41]

The Holy Spirit of Jesus came at Pentecost so that believers might enter into a personal union with him, have their minds illumined to understand the real meaning of his life, teaching and mission, and begin "feeling *already* the powers of the new creation."[42] Luke, who writes from the viewpoint of a second generation Christian, and had himself experienced a personal union with the risen Jesus, wishes to show how others also, as the first apostles, may experience such an encounter. Paul, likewise, insists that the subjugation of this present world has begun. Beker and others assert that the apocalyptic is "not a peripheral curiosity for Paul but the central climate and focus of his thought."[43] Salvation is no longer a matter of *future* expectation alone. Believers now are living in the "overlap" of the old age and the new.

The resurrection of Jesus and the Pentecostal gift of the Spirit make the church an eschatological community "no less now than at its beginning."[44] The Latin words *adventus* and *futurum* point to "the advent of the glorious kingdom of God that is even now coming" and "the future that is yet to come."[45] The present and future are present together but not the same. The church's full participation in the resurrection of Christ is *not yet* but still to come. As such, the church,

> must "remember" the future, which has already come and which will come, and which gives shape and meaning to both the past and the present. Not only because it hopes for the kingdom's

---

40. Moltmann, "Blessing of Hope," 155.
41. Moltmann, "Blessing of Hope," 150.
42. Moltmann, "Presence of God's Future," 579.
43. Beker, *Paul the Apostle*, 144.
44. Mostert, "The Kingdom Anticipated," 37.
45. Anderson, *Ministry on the Fireline*, 194.

coming in its fullness, but also because the eschatological reality of God's salvation and sovereign rule is already real in an anticipatory way in the church.[46]

It is the end that defines and shapes the present by its *in-breaking* presence. It is "the end that is determinative, not the beginning" and "the beginning is reckoned from him who is at the end, and who is that end."[47] God works in the present to renew, restore, and transform, rather than replace, as he did with the body of Jesus.[48] The church's proclamation of the resurrection is meaningful only because "the resurrection itself begins the history of the freeing of human beings and the whole sighing creation from the forces of annihilation and death."[49]

The participants all indicate experiences of, and an ongoing expectation of, God's eschatological salvation, or in-breaking, in their lives through the action of the Holy Spirit. Each indicates that their true identity is found in the future but appropriated in the present through the action of the Holy Spirit. When Emma was born again, she loved Jesus, understood the power of God, and knew that God had a better life, plan, and purpose for her. Sophia understands herself to be close to Jesus and the Holy Spirit. For her, Jesus is indwelling, and the kingdom is within her. She talks about a power we need to tap into. Scarlett refers to being filled with the Holy Spirit. Adam refers to a new life in Christ, being baptized in the Holy Spirit, and knowing that God is with him. Julian talks of being prophesied over.[50] Chloe says that God gave her an amazing vision that described her future ministry, and later had a three-day experience in the Holy Spirit. Julian speaks of feeling and sensing the presence of God.

Conclusion

This chapter has sought to show the Christian community of faith as a movement originating from God, which provides the context for the ongoing work of the Spirit who is shaping a way of being and living in the world that progressively conforms to the person of Christ, and where the

---

46. Anderson, *Ministry on the Fireline*, 194.
47. Knight, *Eschatological Economy*, 15–16.
48. Wright, *Resurrection of the Son*, 372.
49. Moltmann, *Way of Jesus Christ*, 241.
50. Prophecy is one of the *charismata* given by the Spirit (see 1 Cor 12:1–7; 14:1–3).

power of the Spirit is bringing progressive liberation and freedom which will be complete when the kingdom of God has fully come. In discussing the selected interpretative themes ideographically, and the meta-themes nomothetically, it can be seen that believers hold that their lives have been touched and are being changed through the outreaching, upbuilding, and transformational ministries of the church empowered by the Spirit of the resurrected Christ who is its present and living hope.

7

HEALING

Introduction

THIS CHAPTER WILL ADDRESS the experience of the human self in encounter and relationship with the divine. The primary interest here is how this human-divine relationship affects therapeutic benefits which are transformational and healing. The interpretative themes addressed are depth and need; facilitators to healing; remembering and understanding; disclosing abuse; naming abuse; inhibitors and relapses; trust and safety; forgiveness and healing; identity and purpose; and healing and wholeness.

Remembering and Understanding

Chloe

Chloe's memories of her abuse were recovered in adulthood. Looking back, she feels her appearance affected the perpetrator. A three-day encounter with God brought understanding with regard to her difficulties with sex, initiated disclosure, and began the process of recovery. Remembering and understanding the abuse enabled her to realize that it wasn't an innate problem with her. She now understands the abuse in terms of something having been stolen from her. Telling her husband helped him understand the real dynamics in the difficulties in their sexual relationship and bonded them further as a married couple. Disclosure to close friends followed later. Chloe likens disclosure of the abuse to open heart surgery.

Naming Abuse

Scarlett

It took a long time for Scarlett to clearly see that she had been abused. There were subtleties involved that clouded what really happened. The perpetrator continually reinforced the rightness of what was happening. What now seems obvious was then very blurry. At the time she had no idea that his actions were deliberate and intentional. It was very difficult later coming to grips with the malintent of her father. When she did have a flash of insight that it was wrong, she experienced a change in the way she saw what was happening. As Scarlett became aware of, acknowledged, and named her buried feelings, her understanding increased.

Disclosing Abuse

Julian

Julian wanted to disclose the abuse but did not know where it would be right and safe to do so. The first disclosure was at eighteen years of age. Julian felt safe with the person who seemed to be able to see past the façade that all was not well. Disclosing to family members occurred when circumstances facilitated a spontaneous opening up. He felt he needed to talk to his mother before any other family members and that happened naturally in a conversation at about twenty-five years of age. After that, he was able to talk to others about it. When he talked to his younger brother, he noticed he wasn't angry. He understands this to mean that some healing had already happened. When he found his younger brother had been similarly abused by the same person, and that opening up would help his family, he felt the need to talk about it. He believes disclosure in various forms opens the heart for transformation if one is prepared to stay there rather than shut down again.

Depth and Need

Julian

For Julian, the need for intimacy was a deeper issue than the abuse in need of healing. An uncontrollable emotional outpouring of tears brought an inner calmness, clarity of mind, and an experience of God's presence. Julian felt that God cared and understood. Hearing from God meant hearing from deep within and shifted his identity from performance to inner qualities. Afterwards, he was able to connect with people in a more meaningful way and talk about the abuse.

A deeper knowing and relationship with God resulted in a changing perspective on the past. He understood the impact of past events had been mismanaged in denial. Finding his acceptance, value, and identity in God gave rise to an ability to see, question, and eliminate defensive responses from insecurity and a lack of self-acceptance.

He now understood past events and people had had significance in his life. Some people had deeply impacted his life. Deep things happened in unanticipated ways. He now sees that openness facilitated some healing. He was able to share where there was a felt genuine friendliness. He believes that at our core where the Holy Spirit works we are not separated from one another. There is something uniquely valuable in each person. He understands that each person bears a measure of the image of God which is perfect in Christ alone.

Facilitators to Healing

Chloe

Chloe believes that God works through relationships. She understands that God has healed through the attitudes of people in ways not immediately perceptible. A gentle disposition can facilitate healing. People can reinforce a positive self-image. Positive past connections can recover some good childhood feelings. Trusting a male has been important in the healing process. Re-discovering trust has been vital to recovery and ongoing wellness.

Openness to God has facilitated healing. Knowing that God values her has greatly helped. She now recognizes that God only works for her healing, even in trials. The love of her heavenly Father is the antidote to feelings of victimhood. Potentially re-traumatizing comments can be reprocessed. Understanding that healing is a process has been helpful to recovery. Chloe's own healing was a supernatural, miraculous event which needed to be later processed over time.

Inhibitors and Relapses

Chloe

When Chloe was criticized and manipulated by a former supposed trusted relative it resulted in fear and a relapse into the feelings and thoughts of victimhood. Grief from a perceived loss gave way to a lack of insight, deception, and vulnerability to a substitute satisfaction of need. Having lapsed into feelings of victimhood, life seems not worth living. The antidote was a fresh revelation from God. Chloe believes the power of evil to be personal and committed to her destruction, and that the main weapon employed is an attack on her personal worth. Even after recovery, reverting to old and familiar feelings and thoughts is possible. Disappointment can trigger a reversion to the old feelings of worthlessness and helplessness, as well as feelings and thoughts of isolation and self-pity. These are a self-protection mechanism.

While one can be healed of the pain of sexual abuse, the vulnerability to being triggered into reverting to old thoughts and feelings is ever-present. Recovery, after reverting to old feelings, is a particularly long and difficult process. This can only be avoided by consciously relying on God. Without God, victims are likely to develop strongly negative, bitter, and cynical attitudes or resort to homosexual relationships, and might be driven to achieve by way of compensation. It involves the daily practice of spiritual disciplines. It is acceptance rather than denial that facilitates healing. She believes that milder forms of childhood sexual abuse, while equally devastating, may stagnate movement from self-blame to true understanding through underestimation.

Trust and Safety

Emma

Emma's lack of understanding of the fatherhood of God was revealed to her from a direct word of knowledge from another minister. She tried to come to terms with the notion of God as her father through researching Christian literature. Becoming convinced of God as her father being loving, caring, and trustworthy, took a long time. Being at peace in what would have been a formerly terrifying experience indicated to her that she was now trusting God as her father. She describes trusting God as father as the preeminent trust.

Chloe

Chloe understands that a person designated as trustworthy who abuses a child has exploited them, and so trusting comes to mean vulnerability to abuse and pain. This interferes with the ability to trust others. Compliments are interpreted as manipulative. There is also self-blame for trusting the perpetrator. Chloe believes regaining trust is paramount in recovery and ongoing well-being. Re-experiencing a sense of trust was perceived as God restoring an essential which included an appreciated and valued sense of safety.

Chloe believes that trust is more fundamental to relationship than love. Early positive life-experiences were characterized by trust. It is essential to a good and healthy relationship. Sexual abuse violates trust. Self-sacrifice cultivates trust. Her relationship with God is one of trust. He is completely trustworthy. Trusting God means that he is working for good even when the opposite seems to be the case. Faith and trust in God have to be exercised on a daily basis for peace and well-being. Either God is completely trustworthy or not at all. Either God is good and kind or extremely cruel. Trust must be allowed to transcend understanding. Choosing to trust God engenders peace. The only option is to continually trust God. Trust is the only option for dealing with life.

Forgiveness and Healing

Liam

Liam identified the primary issue that needed to be dealt with as forgiveness, which occurred later with the assistance of a pastor. When initially challenged to forgive, he indicated he was unable to. He was challenged to distinguish between inability and unwillingness, and that choosing not to forgive was to put God out of the picture. For the sake of his relationship with God, he became willing to forgive and let go of all judgment.

Identity and Purpose

Emma

Emma came to understand that there was a part of herself inside that was still a child. She believes abused people can sometimes act childishly because there is a child inside them. This inner part of the abused victim needs to come to adulthood. For the childlike part to come to maturity means experiencing the loss of childhood. Letting go of the child within would mean losing her childhood. The greatest difficulty was in allowing the child part of her to depart.

She believes the victim's belief system in relation to themselves and the world is completely erroneous. Healing involved deriving her identity from internalizing God's expressed thoughts about her. She understood that God created her, meaning he designed her for a purpose and knows what her life will hold. This knowledge was all she needed to overcome within. She came to recognize the fact that just because her upbringing was abnormal didn't mean she was. Understanding that her abnormal upbringing didn't dictate her identity was a major thing. Healing primarily involved discovering her true identity in God. She maintains that without discovering that, she would not have recovered. She determined that it was God, and not her abuse, that would dictate the course and quality of her life. There was a determination to not allow her life to be defined by her woundedness.

Emma understands her true identity could only be revealed by the Holy Spirit and exposure to the Word of God. Coming to Christ meant the knowledge that she belonged to God. She needed to understand and appreciate that she wasn't being judged by God. It meant she had become part of a new family. She now understood herself to be defined by whom God said she was. Only God could remove the shame, so other things could also be dealt with.

Healing and Wholeness

Sophia

Sophia believes that God had a purpose for her and empowered her to make forward steps spiritually toward wholeness. That belief provided stability and strength. She understands God could heal miraculously but that her healing had been a process. Healing has involved having the capacity to stop thoughts that negate progress. It involved beginning to understand the priority of understanding her identity in Christ. She understands that, in following the leading of the Spirit and learning to trust, there would be a personal progression toward wholeness. She sees the process of healing to be related to sanctification and the ability to display the fruit of the Spirit.

Liam

Although Liam has questioned God as to why the abuse could happen, he observes that God has been faithful to bring healing. He doesn't see God as responsible for the abuse, and so asking why God allowed it to happen is unproductive as some things just happen. He sees one key to healing as allowing God to do what he wants to do over time. He understands healing to be a process where God is working in a number of areas in a number of ways and at different rates. Opening up, while beneficial, was only the beginning of a process of healing. He likens the beginning of healing to the opening up of a wound so that cleansing can start. While he wanted instant recovery, he now sees the wisdom of God working to bring healing progressively in his life in a variety of ways over time. Healing over time, rather than instantly, produces spiritual growth. God progressively has worked to form his life and character. Healing and growth are like going to the gym: they involve a commitment to repetition to receive progress.

Summary

The idiographic representations of interpretative themes which related to the recovered victims' experiences of themselves in the presence of the divine, as identified in the transcripts, have yielded a number of deeper categories of meaning which I will discuss nomothetically in the three meta-themes in this chapter. I have entitled these meta-themes: human knowing as transformative; human love as supportive of a deeper knowing; and, intimacy in God's love as healing.

Human Knowing as Transformative

Polyani's *eikonic eclipse* and Meek's *two-dimensional glasses* are references to a defective outlook, our *default mode*, where "one's sense of a problem tends to be cut down or trained to fit what can be intellectualized"[1]—and which "prevents us from seeing the central transformative role of the imagination in rationality."[2] Information, facts, statements, and formulas are not all there is to human knowing. To know is to be on the way, where progress "is not linear as much as it is repeatedly unfolding and transforming."[3] According to Loder, transformation

> does not merely refer to change in a positive direction . . . Rather, transformation occurs whenever, within a given frame of reference or experience, hidden orders of coherence and meaning emerge to replace or alter the axioms of a given frame and reorder its elements accordingly.[4]

In light of this Barker says,

> Clearly, transformation is not more of the same, but a fundamental reconfiguration or resignification of the component parts of a given situation. Transformation always involves a perceptual shift, which is often requisite for the resolution of a conflicted situation. This is true for both psychosocial and existential-spiritual frames of experience.[5]

Conflicts which are *psychosocial* and/or *existential-spiritual* in nature require transformation if resolution is to occur. Each *transforming moment* involves an insight which opens up a whole new perspective and a way forward. These moments of transformation are bracketed by previous preparatory moments and subsequent responsive moments. Loder calls these "the grammar of the knowing event."[6] Whether the context is that of sci-

---

1. Polyani, *Personal Knowledge*, 46.
2. Meek, *Loving to Know*, 470.
3. Meek, *Loving to Know*, 35.
4. Loder, *Transforming Moment*, 229.
5. Barker, "Relevance of James Loder's Grammar," 160.
6. Loder, *Transforming Moment*, 42–43.

entific inquiry, religious conversion, or psychotherapy, beneath the varied and manifold expressions of transformation at the surface is found "a deep, underlying pattern" which is common to each. This *logic* or *grammar* of transformation structures regardless of content. Loder says, "It is innate to want completion of transformational logic wherever it appears, just as we want completion of any recognizable sentence or any narrative form."[7]

Within the therapeutic context, transformational knowing reveals "a patterned process of healing" where "the self itself undergoes transformation."[8] Loder explains the healing process as "essentially a knowing event working transformationally on defences and the conflicts buried beneath them."[9] The first step in the process of therapeutic knowing is articulating the conflict. Initially, this may mean struggling to describe certain feelings for which there are not yet any clear concepts.

Chloe was conflicted over sex as God's gift being really difficult, painful, and something she hated. Scarlett was really surprised by how much effect the abuse had on later sexual experiences with her husband. Emma was stunned and conflicted to see herself standing in front of herself, covered in blackness, and hearing the Spirit say, "It's you." After Julian's sister asked him for the third or fourth time, "Are you OK?," he wept uncontrollably and didn't understand why. Though Liam felt his sexual experiences were strange and abnormal, he initially didn't know it. Sophia started hearing songs about Abba Father, and yet she initially felt he was fickle. The participants' experiences indicate *ruptures* in their knowing which were sometimes recognized and able to be articulated, and sometimes unrecognized and only articulated after a deeper conflict was realized.

The second step in therapeutic knowing is "an interlude for scanning." Loder says,

> To be temporarily baffled over a conflict in one's situation is to be drawn both consciously and unconsciously into the familiar psychological process of searching out the possible solutions, taking apart errors, keeping parts, and discarding others . . . Scanning is not only a search for answers outside the problem; it is also scanning and differentiating the terms of the problem and playing

---

7. Loder, *Transforming Moment*, 42.
8. Loder, *Transforming Moment*, 57.
9. Loder, *Transforming Moment*, 57.

possible solutions against various interpretations of the ruptured situation.[10]

The various separate elements and associations around the conflict are scanned for implicit patterns and new ways of connecting into a richer and more healing whole, wherein the conflict is resolved, bringing relief. Julian's conflict of "Why can't I be healed of this?," when God can heal these things, led to further asking "Where's my faith?"; "What kind of faith do I need?"; "How do I get that faith?"; and thinking, "Maybe this and that will help my life." He describes this time as a dialogue in which he was enduring a paradox of God, involving comments like, "I shouldn't have to . . ."; "I should be able to . . ."; "You can . . ."; "If you are . . ."; and "Why can't this be . . .?" Emma describes the process of moving from "Where was God?" to realizing that God loved her as a huge step. Liam assessed his inability to forgive against his understanding of what God wanted. Resolving to forgive brought an unexpected sense of relief. Scarlett indicates that trusting God as Father is something that came over time slowly.

The third step in therapeutic knowing is insight, something intuitively experienced, a "constructive act of the imagination." Loder states,

> an insight, intuition, or vision appears on the border between the conscious and the unconscious, usually with convincing force, and conveys in a form readily available to the consciousness the essence of the resolution.[11]

Meek says, "The knowing event issues in a sense that we have made contact with reality."[12] It is accredited as real because "we have a sense of the possibility of indeterminate future manifestations."[13] Barker describes this step as when "the disconnected and individually known elements are reconnected in a new and healing way."[14]

This insight seems to emerge spontaneously and with compelling power. All participants indicate moments of insight which hold the promise of resolution. Liam says, "Once . . . I realized that . . . it wasn't normal . . . that was a real relief." When Sophia had a word for the black mass that was churning over inside, then it was OK. The wrongness of the abuse came as a

10. Loder, *Transforming Moment*, 37–38.
11. Loder, *Transforming Moment*, 38.
12. Meek, *Loving to Know*, 75.
13. Meek, *Loving to Know*, 75
14. Barker, "Relevance of James Loder's Grammar," 161.

sudden flash to Scarlett. Julian couldn't explain why the words "I don't want to die" came to him until, in a vision, he saw himself as a little boy after his father's death saying, "I want to die." When Emma was delivered of "a spirit of rejection," she understood what the black spots were. Chloe remembered and realized, "Yes, it did happen to me." Adam describes linking two, seemingly unrelated, abusive situations in his life as making the connection.

The fourth stage of the process is constituted by a release and redirection of energy. Energy bound up in sustaining the conflict is released as the unconscious responds to the resolution. The new context of knowing is the opening of the conscious for a measure of self-transcendence.[15] Loder says, "consciousness is expanded by, and to the measure of, the resolution."[16] Ratcliff says, "the tension built in the first two phases is now released because of the *insight* achieved and consequent re-patterning of the original conflict."[17]

All seven recovered victims experienced insights relating to their abuse that brought both relief and another focus. When Scarlett realized that "when a woman says *no* she means *no*," she was released from the power of her father's lie. When Liam responded to the realization that he needed to forgive, it was like a weight off his shoulders and feeling like he could then face life. After Chloe realized what had happened, she wondered what it would mean. Julian identified a deeper need within, and so discovered a deeper person. Sophia experienced times of sobbing at home from insights gained through reading testimonial stories. When Adam found that similar abuse had happened to others, his view of his own experience changed. After her unexpected deliverance, Emma's mind was changed.

The fifth step in therapeutic knowing is *interpretation*. In this stage, the meaning of the insight is clarified and confirmed. Insight is both tested for *coherence* and *correspondence*. The insight must be clearly connected to the original conflict and correspond to a consensus view of the world. All seven recovered victims interpret their healing as being from God.

Scarlett understands she no longer has panic attacks because God healed her. She understands her overall healing as a spiritual journey and a gradual thing because if everything happened all at once, it would not be possible "to walk in the fullness of it." The beauty of the Holy Spirit is that he does not push victims "to take on any more than . . . [they] can

---

15. Loder, *Transforming Moment*, 38–39.
16. Loder, *Transforming Moment*, 38–39.
17. Ratcliff, "Qualitative Data Analysis," 117.

cope with at any one time." Liam understands that healing comes from a relationship with God, and "God being faithful to bring healing." Chloe interprets her three-day experience in the Holy Spirit as "God . . . doing a surgery" and "short-circuiting the healing." Julian refers to healing as a process and a journey of being able to understand better who he is and who God created him to be. He contrasts how he feels now with how it was then, and attributes the difference to "God's healing hand in the process." Sophia recalls that prior to experiencing healing, she was stuck in pain, and every memory was really painful and "a really raw place to be." She maintains that God is the healer. Adam indicates that the most important thing in healing is knowing that God is with you. Emma understands her healing to be in finding her identity in God and maintains that she wouldn't have been healed any other way.

Loder makes a distinction between two-dimensional and four-dimensional transforming moments, and between the power of the human and Holy Spirit.[18] The first two dimensions relate to normal development and consist of "the lived world" and "the self." Meaning is both supplied by our environment and constructed by us in our interaction with that environment. Thus, human beings have an innate potential to resolve psychosocial conflicts. The human spirit empowers the movement through the grammar and is the source of the creative resolutions of psychosocial conflicts. All seven recovered victims indicate secular counseling to be insufficient in bringing healing from the trauma of childhood sexual abuse.

The human spirit cannot rectify the *fallenness* of human beings or resolve conflicts that are existential-spiritual in nature. With respect to these, it is the Holy Spirit who is the source and power that moves a person through the grammar of transformation. All seven recovered victims refer to the therapeutic benefits of counseling dependent upon the presence and direction of the Holy Spirit. Receiving the Spirit's resolution is not the same as constructing one's own resolution. In existential-spiritual conflicts, the human's spirit role is that of openness to the transforming presence and direction of the Holy Spirit. Loder refers to this as "convictional knowing," which is a deeper and even more transformative experience.[19]

Convictional knowing involves two further dimensions to human existence beyond the ego's capacity and limits: the void and the Holy. The *void* is "the possibility of annihilation, the potential and eventually inevitable

---

18. Loder, *Transforming Moment*, 114.
19. Loder, *Transforming Moment*, 93–122.

absence of one's being . . . implicit in existence from birth and explicit in death."[20] Loder says this third dimension of being "has many faces," such as "absence, loss, shame, guilt, hatred, loneliness and the demonic."[21] But the first two dimensions alone are incapable of overcoming it. Being confronted with weakness, finitude and death mean living with despair or experiencing "the transformation of all transformations, the negation of the negation, which can only come from *being-itself* experienced as gracious— the Holy."[22] The *Holy* is "an undoing of nothingness."[23] It is "that which is unique, set apart, and manifest as new being, reversing and overcoming annihilation, express[ing] . . . the graciousness of being-itself."[24]

Christian faith sees *being-itself* interpreted as God manifest in Jesus Christ. In Christ, being-itself enters the void and negates sin, and then rises to negate the negation. Fowler interpreting Loder says, "Christ's double negation works a double negation in which self, world, void and the Holy are now all seen through the lens of Christ."[25] Encounter with Christ as the fourth dimension is the way of transformation.

Human Love as Supportive of Deeper Knowing

Rahner maintains that knowledge is ordained to fulfillment in love. He says, "In the heart of knowledge stands love, from which knowledge itself lives."[26] He speaks of love as "the light of knowledge" and knowledge as "the luminous radiance of love." Meek says, "The real behaves like a person. Treat it personally and it will respond personally."[27] What motivates the inquiry after knowledge is a longing after truth, not for information but transformation. It involves love: a caring and attentiveness, an imaginative summoning of future possibilities and flourishing, and readiness for a mutual indwelling or communion with reality. When received, it is

---

20. Loder, *Transforming Moment*, 70.
21. Loder, *Transforming Moment*, 84.
22. Loder, *Conversations on Fowler's Stages of Faith and Loder's the Transforming Moment*, 142.
23. Loder, *Transforming Moment*, 70.
24. Loder, *Transforming Moment*, 70–71.
25. Loder and Fowler, "Conversations on Fowler's Stages," 142.
26. Rahner, *Hearer of the Word*, 83.
27. Meek, *Loving to Know*, 427.

HEALING

transformative *"because it expresses itself faithfully."* Referring to Loder's account of knowing, Meek says,

> The knower responds to conflict in context by seeking a deeper coherence that will restore equilibrium. The more one cares about the conflict, the more powerful the knowing event will be . . . in fact, one cannot come to know what one does not care about.[28]

For Polyani, Loder, and Meek, the *interlude of scanning* (Loder) or the *creative imagination* and *intuition* (Polyani), which guides the knower to the solution with increasing proximity, means the conflicted situation is indwelt with empathy for the problem. The release of energy and re-patterning of the "aha" moment "is the opening of her- or himself up to the resolution."[29] Meek holds that knowing is transformative,

> precisely because its dynamic is interpersonal . . . what transforms us, in our knowing, is not a what but a who. This . . . is . . . personed features of the yet-to-be-known.[30]

Knowing anything involves "mutual indwelling,"[31] and means "to indwell it and reconstruct it in one's own terms without losing the essence of what is being indwelt."[32] The knower contemplates,

> . . . a wave of related new associations, carrying the implications further than the original conflict suggested and thereby immersing the knower more richly and deeply than ever in his or her [new] assumptional.[33]

Meek claims that "knowing as transformational is also healing."[34]

In psychotherapy, whether pastoral or secular, both the therapist and the client/parishioner are mutually involved in a process of coming to new knowledge. Clough maintains that, "Therapy generally begins with developing a relationship and subsequently problem-solving."[35] For Rogers, it

---

28. Meek, *Loving to Know*, 124.
29. Meek, *Loving to Know*, 125.
30. Meek, *Loving to Know*, 136–37.
31. Meek, *Loving to Know*, 128.
32. Loder, *Transforming Moment*, 30.
33. Loder, *Transforming Moment*, 38–39.
34. Meek, *Loving to Know*, 126–27. Meek believes that Loder confirms this with regard to therapeutic knowing.
35. Clough, "To Be Loved," 23.

was not problem-solving, but genuineness, empathy, and unconditional positive regard that were central to the process of therapy and which allowed the genuine person to emerge.[36] These core conditions have been recognized as the provision of love in the therapeutic process.[37] Many authors argue that love is essential for being human.[38] Human development theorists have widely acknowledged the need for love in child development.[39] However, it was Rogers who placed the need for love at the core of the human experience and personal growth.

Rogers believed persons could find healing within themselves if they could find certain qualities within the therapist. A person could grow and change in an environment of empathetic understanding and unconditional positive regard. He held the longing to be affirmed was rooted in a natural tendency to grow toward health. This was understood as an internal God-given motivation and a *directional tendency* in the universe.[40] Loder attributes this to *the human* spirit which is "a powerful drive, endowed with energy and determination in the face of persistent obstacles to its expansion."[41] This transcending outward move is simultaneously "an inward move, reinforcing one's sense of self."[42]

This *growth tendency*, or motivation to seek health and wholeness, is best facilitated in an environment of empathetic understanding, congruence, and unconditional positive regard. Love assists persons to say and feel everything they need to say and feel. Empathic moments facilitate the creative capacities of the human spirit, within its capacities, to create meaningful solutions. Doehring says, "Often empathy is experienced as a moment in which we simultaneously feel intensely present and able to transcend what is happening."[43] These moments are not the result of "a mechanical process" that can be learnt and applied from a book; they come about

> when we have experienced profound relatedness in which our experiences resonate with the experiences of others in ways that

---

36. Rogers, *Counseling and Psychotherapy*.
37. Thorne, *Person-Centred Counselling*.
38. Fromm, *Art of Loving*; Rogers, "Necessary and Sufficient Conditions"; Maslow, *Motivation and Personality*.
39. Klein, "The Origins of Transference;" Winnicott, *Therapeutic Consultations*.
40. Rogers, *A Way of Being*.
41. Loder, *Logic of Spirit*, 33.
42. Loder, *Logic of Spirit*, 34.
43. Doehring, *Taking Care*, 100.

Healing

allow us to see and feel the depths of these experiences without being overwhelmed.[44]

Benner writes that,

> Dialogue is one of the deepest forms of soul engagement we can experience with another person . . . [it] can never be manufactured, only nurtured and . . . when we do receive the gift of receiving another person in a place of genuine dialogue, we participate in one of life's richest blessings . . . Dialogue is richer than simply conversation . . . In dialogue I attempt to share how I experience the world and seek to understand how you do so. In this process each participant touches and is touched by others. This results in each person's being changed.[45]

The recovered victims refer to such experiences in their healing journey. Julian always had a close relationship with pastors. He felt able to talk about experiences and life at a deeper level with them. He felt drawn into those relationships. Nouwen says, "the minister . . . is a host who offers hospitality . . . a friendly space . . . an empty space where the guest can find his soul."[46] When Julian travelled in the car together with a friend, he found he connected and felt she understood. He maintains she "didn't have to understand to understand." He felt that "someone has actually seen past this exterior," "someone has actually seen that I'm not OK." Though it was painful, there was peace within it, and it was safe to go there. He understands there was a spiritual component to that. Reflecting on sharing with his mother, he understands that it's how they respond to each other that's important. When he doesn't feel rejected, and feels the person is engaged, it "frees up the spirit," and he feels free in that place. Julian says, "It's like a two-way thing . . . that's the dynamics of getting out of this place."

Adam described the prayer counseling he received as opening up with another person who had to be extraordinarily confidential and "together in themselves." Pastoral counseling means "you build a relationship of trust," so as to slowly bring up things that happened, and "try and deal with them by prayer." For Liam, talking about it with the elders at church was the start of shedding light to the reality of things, and healing, which still took time.

Scarlett first opened up to a couple with whom she had befriended, because she felt she could talk with them about it. When she talked to her

---

44. Doehring, *Taking Care*, 102–03.
45. Benner, *Sacred Companions*, 54–55.
46. Nouwen, *The Wounded Healer*, 92.

siblings, it brought them closer together. Reflecting on her husband's understanding, Chloe says God has been her healer, ultimately, but he has worked through her husband to reach her. She likens him to Jesus in that he never pushed.

Emma describes healing as "a knowing." She holds psychologists can teach really good things and people can learn how to change their behavior, but she doesn't believe that they are ever really whole, because they need to know love and know that God loves them so much. She refers to this as "a knowing touched by the Spirit of God," where one touch can change a person's life. Conversely, Sophia first went to someone whom she thought was a mature woman in the church but found that she hadn't been healed and was in a bad place herself. The woman "blustered around" and made Sophia feel embarrassed. Sophia decided she would not come back again.

Humanistic theorists have focused on the role of authenticity, genuineness, and empathetic understanding in the counseling relationship. Psychoanalytic theorists have concentrated on holding[47] and containing[48] in the development of the true self. Behavioral schools speak of positive reinforcement.[49] But all concede that love is fundamental to human experience. The different manifestations of love express a broad range of emotions. Tillich described love as the moving power of life.[50] Peck defines love as "the will to extend oneself for the purpose of nurturing one's own or another's spiritual growth."[51] Siegel says, "the truth is: love heals."[52] Crabb is convinced that communities of faith have the potential to be healing communities where "ordinary Christians whose lives really intersect will accomplish most of the good that . . . now . . . mental health professionals . . . provide.[53]

Manifestations of human love call people to deeper places of trust and connection, but in themselves fail to deliver what the human spirit is

---

47. Winnicott, *Therapeutic Consultations*.

48. Bion, *Elements of Psychoanalysis*.

49. Skinner, "Teaching Machines," 969–77; Beck, *Cognitive Therapy of Depression*.

50. Tillich, *Love, Power and Justice*. These include acceptance, empathy, affection, and compassion to the deepest active relationship.

51. Peck, *The Road Less Travelled*, 85.

52. Siegel, *Love, Miracles and Medicine*, 181. Siegel says, "If I told patients to raise their blood level of immune globulins or killer T cells, no one would know how. But if I can teach them to love themselves and others fully, the same change happens automatically. The truth is: love heals."

53. Crabb, *Connecting*, xii.

Healing

ultimately searching for. The human spirit as transformational will "always point beyond itself" in search of the "ultimate form" of perfect, unconditional, and agapic love.[54] Proximate forms of love "will always be marked by the dark side of human development from which the human spirit by itself cannot extricate itself."[55] The "health-inducing potential" that exists in the love exchanged between people is indicative of "the cosmic presence of divine love existing in the world as a reflection of the nature of the Creator."[56]

While the human spirit has "a measure of constructive power," it is incapacitated by its separation from "its ultimate ground in the Spirit of God."[57] Human love is "a bit of the *imago dei* written into our lives and into the fabric of the universe."[58] But while humans can practice the art of loving,[59] they can never bear the weight of the need for divine love. Parents, friends, and therapists all fail to deliver a perfect love which is completely trustworthy.

Nonetheless, human love supports a deeper knowing and transformation and can teach about divine love. Benner says, "human love always carries enough of its source within it that it retains something of the healing and growth-inducing potential of divine love."[60] Furthermore, the relative constancy of the love of family, friends, therapists, and carers makes the absolute faithfulness of divine love at least conceivable and, possibly, tentatively trustworthy.

Sophia was impacted by some people's consistent good behavior. They never yelled, hit, lied, shamed, or humiliated. She repeats, "they were just so consistent . . . very, very consistent," and "there wasn't a falseness about them." They were genuine. She was drawn to them because they felt safe.

---

54. Loder, *Logic of Spirit*, 10, 269, 321. Interestingly, in a senior thesis done at Princeton University entitled *The Influence of Grandparents on Young Adults*, Tina Horner found 95 percent of participants reported that their grandparents had been very influential and important in their lives. 88 percent reported that they were important because they offered "unconditional love and support" (cited in Loder, 320–21).

55. Loder, *Logic of Spirit*, 269. Such as eros, phileo, and caritas.

56. Benner, *Surrender to Love*, 81.

57. Loder, *Logic of Spirit*, 10.

58. Clough, "To Be Loved and to Love," 26.

59. Fromm, *The Art of Loving*.

60. Benner, *Surrender to Love*, 81.

Learning limited surrender to relatively trustworthy human beings helps prepare for a more complete surrendering to perfect love.[61]

Intimacy in God's Love as Healing

Loder says, intimacy "refers to the inmost place in oneself at the core of one's identity."[62] Nouwen says, "the great enemy of intimacy" is fear, and "love is its true friend."[63] He defines intimacy as "living in the house of love" and maintains that fear does not create a home.[64] Further, the intimate place, "is not a place made by human hands."[65] While an intimate relationship involves the mutual disclosure of selves as openly as possible, no human person can reach the point of deepest intimacy with another. Loder points out that, while "you may know what it is like to be me . . . you'll never know what it is for *me* to be me."[66] And yet, "one of the deepest longings of the human soul is the longing to be seen," or fully known.[67] Benner says, "in the core of our being we yearn for intimacy."[68] O'Donohue calls this, "the echo of a primal intimacy" because "the soul did not invent itself," but "is a presence from the divine world, where intimacy has no limit or barrier."[69] While true friendship "brings out the true contour of . . . [one's] spirit," "there is no mirror in the world where you can catch a glimpse of your soul."[70] Real intimacy is "a sacred experience" and brings "epistemological integration and healing."[71]

Kierkegaard maintained the primacy of intimacy for the healing of human lives. He says a person *is spirit*, and the spirit is the self, which is

---

61. Conversely, conditional and imperfect love from human beings can make the unconditional and perfect love from God seem unbelievable and untrustworthy.

62. Loder, *Logic of Spirit*, 60.

63. Nouwen, *Lifesigns*, 23.

64. Nouwen, *Lifesigns*, 17–18.

65. Nouwen, *Lifesigns*, 25.

66. Loder, *Logic of Spirit*, 60. Thomas Nagel's essay entitled "What is it Like to be a Bat?" arrives at the realization that "while he can understand what it would be like to be a bat, he could never understand what it would be like for a bat to be a bat."

67. O'Donohue, *Anam Cara*, 49.

68. Benner, *Sacred Companions*, 14.

69. O'Donohue, *Anam Cara*, 49.

70. O'Donohue, *Anam Cara*, 49.

71. O'Donohue, *Anam Cara*, 38–39.

intensely and irreducibly relational. The self is constituted by the relation between two polar aspects becoming "a positive third term," relating itself to itself.[72] Loder holds that, "this dynamic interrelational view of self describes a person as spirit," and that, "it is by the spirit that the inmost core of the person is known (1Cor 2:10–11)."[73] While the human spirit has a capacity to construct and expand horizons of meaning, it has no answer as to why "it should create an environment of trust," "it should go on creating the structures of development," or "it should exist at all."[74] Separated from its source, "it works as ungrounded transformation," giving rise to "a random sense of freedom."[75] For Kierkegaard, the equilibrium of the self is maintained only as the self relates itself to that power which constituted the relation. When "the self is grounded transparently in the Power which posited it," despair or "disrelationship," sin, and the absence of intimacy, is eliminated.[76]

Loder finds an *analogia spiritus* between human beings and the divine being. What the human spirit is to humanity, the Holy Spirit is to God. The human spirit is rooted and grounded in the human soul; the Holy Spirit is rooted and grounded in God. Furthermore, the human and divine Spirit are made for each other. They are "interrelated" according to "the bipolar relationality" which constitutes "the relational wholeness of Jesus Christ."[77] The Spirit offers to replicate this same relational wholeness in human beings, calling the human spirit "home," away from futility and perversity and into the communion of the Trinity.

God is both Spirit and relational love and, as such, is "trinitarianly knowable."[78] The Father is known through the Son in the Spirit. This Spirit-to-spirit intimacy constitutes the human self in God as a child of God (Rom 8:16), and liberates the human spirit to be itself, without losing its distinctiveness. It "runs deeper than any human intimacies," and is definitive of them.[79] Nouwen understands the mystery of the incarnation to mean that,

---

72. Kierkegaard, *Sickness unto Death*.
73. Loder, "The Great Sex Charade," 84.
74. Kierkegaard, *Sickness unto Death*, 118.
75. Kierkegaard, *Sickness unto Death*, 36.
76. Kierkegaard, *Sickness unto Death*, 10, 11.
77. Loder, *Logic of Spirit*, 36.
78. Gunton, *Act and Being*, 110.
79. Loder, *Logic of Spirit*, 60.

> Jesus, in whom the fullness of God dwells, has become our home. By making his home in us he allows us to make our home in him. By entering into the intimacy of our innermost self he offers us the opportunity to enter into his own intimacy with God. By choosing us as *his* preferred dwelling place he invites us to choose him as *our* preferred dwelling place.[80]

O'Donohue says, "In friendship with him we enter the tender beauty and affection of the Trinity, in the embrace of this eternal friendship we dare to be free."[81]

This supreme intimacy means a person knows they are loved by God. Loder maintains it is precisely at this deepest point where one is touched by the spiritual presence of Christ that one recognizes "with profound suddenness" and "lasting effect" that "the Spirit of Christ knows better than I do what it means for me to be me."[82] He says,

> this transformational impact of the divine Spirit thereby connects with the depth and power of my innermost being and makes me know what it means for me to be irretrievably spiritual . . . once I am at this level of personal depth, there are . . . irreversible consequences. Once wised up at this point, there is no wising down.[83]

Pure or perfect love comes to life in the human person through the Spirit and is transformational in its character and power. Being known by God, which Rosner argues is equivalent to knowing oneself to belong to God, to be loved or chosen by God, and to be a child or son of God, "promotes humility and supplies comfort and security" thus enabling intimacy at other levels.[84] Rosner maintains, "God's omniscience means that *what we are* is known to God, God's relational knowledge means that *who we are* is known to God."[85] Rosner and McLean argue there are psycho-spiritual benefits to being known in this deeply intimate way by God. They maintain that

> secure attachment to the Transcendent One, being known by God as His child, supplies a strong sense of a valuable and lovable self.

---

80. Nouwen, *Wounded Healer*, 25.
81. O'Donohue, *Anam Cara*, 37.
82. Loder, "The Great Sex Charade," 83.
83. Loder, "The Great Sex Charade," 83.
84. Rosner, "Known by God," 207.
85. Rosner, "Known by God," 209.

Healing

> Similar to the human parent-child relationship, such attachment can lead to a healthy sense of significance, offer an effective source of comfort in dispirited circumstances, and give moral direction.[86]

Research indicates that "knowing that one is loved and lovable underlies the secure state of mind that promotes well-being and protects against illness."[87] They further maintain,

> The experience of not being abandoned in our suffering, the sense that two are present in the terror or the pain, that one is not forgotten but is instead held in mind, appears to be one of the quintessential requirements for the resolution of loss and trauma and for the reestablishment of a strong self.[88]

The intimacy of the parent-child relationship is fundamental to a child's identity and well-being. However, as Loder asserts, "the supreme intimacy occurs by the power of God's Spirit at work in one's innermost self, by one who knows one is loved by God."[89] This love "redefines life."[90] Divine, pure love is, and offers, an "absolute unity of being."[91]

The seven recovered victims' spiritual and healing journeys disclose the categories of coming to know about God, a personal relationship with God, and a deeper realization, yielding to, and trusting in, the intimacy of being fully known, in present and eternal time, and unconditionally loved. All the participants had a personal relationship with God prior to finding healing in yielding to a deeper intimacy. All of the participants refer to this as an experience with the Holy Spirit.

Scarlett feels she has experienced more God than other people who haven't needed such a degree of healing. Liam was very emotional to realize that God was working at a deeper level, in a way he wasn't expecting. He can't imagine healing without God. Chloe says, "God had to become very intimate to me." For Sophia, every time God reached out to her, she was able move on from one stage to the next.

Julian equates the journey of healing to "being able to understand better who I am—who God created me to be." He talks of himself in terms of

---

86. Rosner and McLean, "Theology and Human Flourishing," 65.
87. Rosner and McLean, "Theology and Human Flourishing," 72.
88. Rosner and McLean, "Theology and Human Flourishing," 78.
89. Loder, *Logic of Spirit*, 252.
90. Loder, *Logic of Spirit*, 276.
91. Loder, *Logic of Spirit*, 276.

the person who "tried to find every sort of quick fix." But when it comes to the true person God created him to be, he describes himself as "the person in tune with the Spirit." He understands that those places in him which were crying out were invitations for the Spirit to work. For Julian, only the Spirit's presence is safe, enabling him to go deeper, as deep as he wants to, without feeling judged or guilty. Julian feels the abuse exposed a deeper need for a real sense of intimacy. This is where he believes the healing was taking place.

Emma got it into her spirit that it was what God thinks and says about her that defined who she really was. God knew her before she was formed in her mother's womb. She found she could really trust him and wanted to get God's perception on things because her perception was warped. To realize that God knew her caused her to be unconcerned about what other people thought. When she got hold of the love of God, everything else had to go. Emma realized that it all came back to believing, "You are everything that he says about you."

Adam found that new life in Christ motivated and required him to deal with his stuff. He received prayer counseling, which was really valuable. It involved opening up "under the power of the Spirit to God"; "getting everything out"; praying; and being forgiven. He believes that one of the ways through sexual abuse is describing what happened, "talking it out," and "finding a way . . . to forgive the person who has abused." He believes healing involves "dealing with everything in your life that isn't of God." This involves and requires a trustworthy support system; "knowing that God is with you as you sort it out"; and "knowing that sorting it out will mean bringing it up over and over again and that God is still with you over and over again." It means "knowing that in the end, it will be alright," and that "in the end, it's alright with God."

Conclusion

In this chapter I have sought to address the therapeutic benefits for the human person in the presence of the divine being, whom Christians refer to as the triune God, or, the Father, the Son, and the Holy Spirit. This chapter has sought to address the nature of the beneficial changes experienced by the participants in their healing journeys. I have found that they have experienced therapeutic benefits from a relationship with God, but also in relationship with people, where those relationships mirrored something of the divine. I have also found that the deepest healing transformations occurred when there was openness, trust, and expectancy to the perfectly knowing and unconditionally loving presence of God. For them, this intimate spiritual union with God revealed their true identity, value, and purpose, and brought healing transformation.

8

THE HOLY SPIRIT

Introduction

IN THIS CHAPTER I will discuss the work of the Holy Spirit in bringing healing to victims of childhood sexual abuse. The interpretive themes dealt with are the flame of the Spirit; interventions and interruptions; revelation and change; event and process; infilling of the Holy Spirit; guidance and counseling; overwhelming help from the Spirit; and the Spirit and Christ.

The Flame of the Spirit

Sophia

Sophia describes her childhood conversion as the igniting of a flame in her spirit. Receiving Christ meant receiving ongoing help from the Holy Spirit. She has never doubted the personal presence and care of Jesus. She believes the Spirit brought protection and change into her life. He protected her internally. He gave her the strength to stop further and worse abuse. He prompted thoughts consistent with the will of God. He also deposited more potential into her life than she then realized. Her lack of anger as a child is attributed to the Spirit. When she prayed for God to remove her constant nightmares, they stopped, and she slept peacefully.

Sophia now understands that the inner candle of the Spirit can be increased. She has been so full of the Holy Spirit that she looked to be drunk and some normal functions were difficult to carry out. Intermittent in-fillings of the Holy Spirit took place regularly over a year. She describes the experience of speaking in tongues as making her feel good, and as a spiritual force against demonic powers. She highlights the importance of the supernatural intervention of the Spirit.

Interventions and Interruptions

Emma

Emma believes God intervened in her life to rescue her from brokenness. Without God's intervention, she would have been an emotional mess. Without God, she would have been completely alone. God had always helped her, even in difficult circumstances.

At one period in her life, it seemed God was unrelenting in pursuing her. While inebriated, she was unexpectedly interrupted by the voice of God, who indicated his desire to bring real meaning and purpose into her life. She agreed and her perspective on things immediately began to change. She experienced hope, and a new sense of purpose, value, and confidence.

She was never angry at God, as she understood that God's heart was to redeem. She knew that God had interrupted and re-directed her life and that she loved him. It was now God, and not her abuse, that dictated and determined the course of her life. Emma believes, in order to fulfill her call in helping others, God had to first help her.

Revelation and Change

Emma

Emma understands her regular weeping during church services, over the course of a year, was because God was healing her by uncovering wounds. On one occasion, the Holy Spirit suddenly revealed her true condition to her. She saw herself covered in blackness, which the Spirit indicated was rejection, hatred, injustice, and shame. She had not realized how much she suffered from rejection. Later, she was unexpectedly delivered from "a demonic spirit of rejection," through a "word of knowledge," bringing major change. She holds that not all victims will need deliverance from a spirit of rejection, but if they do, counseling will prove insufficient.

Emma's healing has consisted in God showing her things to be dealt with. A word of knowledge indicated her complete lack of understanding of the Father. The Spirit radically and instantly adjusts her thinking to what is right, by intercepting her train of thought, to bring the needed correction. She describes hearing the voice of the Spirit as "a knowing touched by the Spirit of God." Being open to the Spirit meant receiving a radically different perspective on life. She understands the Holy Spirit to be the primary expert for change in our lives. It is the revelation of God's love to her by the Spirit that has brought the greatest transformation. God has opened her eyes and beautified her life.

Event and Process

Sophia

Sophia believes that while God can and does perform miracles, he communicated to her that healing would be a process over time. She recalls that even after many powerful encounters with the Holy Spirit, there was the understanding that there was more healing that needed to happen. A lot of the healing from God was related to the younger internal fragmented parts that were carrying the impact of the abuse. Sophia understands that God empowers her to make forward steps spiritually, and in recovery, as part of his eternal purpose for her. He fills holes that would otherwise be empty and purposeless. When God removes pain, it is replaced with a better self-image. The positivity and healing in her life was due to God's grace and favor. Her ongoing relationship with Jesus superseded the pain of the past.

Infilling of the Holy Spirit

Adam

Adam contrasts a previous knowledge about the Holy Spirit to his present experience of him. He describes the infilling of the Holy Spirit as the "blooming" of every part of his inner being, and totally life-changing. He describes it as the lighting of an internal fire which had an overflowing expression. It created a desire in him for God to fill every part of his life. He understands the Holy Spirit to be God present and moving in people's lives. He holds that receiving, or being filled with the Holy Spirit, only occurs when we "give permission" for him to come. He describes the outcome for his church receiving the Holy Spirit as joy, love, and relationships that worked. He attributes our willingness to admit and confess fault on our part to the Holy Spirit. He understands that while the Spirit "compelled" him to sort out relationships, his cooperation was needed. He believes it is the person of the Holy Spirit who inspires faith and ongoing trust in God. Adam believes the person and power of the Holy Spirit are not understood by most believers, and the power available to us through the Spirit is underestimated.

Guidance and Counseling

Scarlett

For Scarlett there was a great deal of comfort in knowing that the Holy Spirit had directed her to the right counselor, was directing the process, and that growth and learning were taking place. The counseling process involved learning to hear the voice of the Spirit. Each counseling session involved asking for the direction of the Holy Spirit, who would then bring thoughts to her mind in relation to where healing was needed. Sometimes this was not related to sexual abuse. Scarlett asserts that it is wrong to adopt a formulaic approach to healing. While following the voice of the Spirit often involves some cost and sacrifice, it also brings blessing and facilitates healing. Conversely, not heeding the guidance of the Spirit, in counseling persons who have been sexually abused, may result in further damage. The leading of the Spirit is imperative as the Spirit knows the person and the best way and time to move forward. It is learning to trust the Holy Spirit that facilitates healing and further learning.

Adam

Adam understands that the motivation for entering new life in Christ comes from the Holy Spirit. He believes the motivation to find healing through prayer counseling came from the Holy Spirit. He understood that he could address any area of needed change because of the presence of the Holy Spirit in and with him. He describes the counseling ministry he underwent to be a gradual opening up in the conscious, enabling presence of the Holy Spirit, so as to expose every relevant area of his life where healing and change may be necessary. Without the enabling of the Holy Spirit, the pain of the abuse would have remained.

Overwhelming Help from the Spirit

Chloe

Chloe indicates that her healing and freedom from childhood sexual abuse has been through the Holy Spirit alone. During a three-day experience of being filled with the Spirit, she had vivid and detailed memories of her abuse. It involved intermittent periods of crying, laughing, and sleeping, lasting for hours. During this time, issues were brought up and dealt with. The memories explained her present difficulties with sex and led to her disclosing the incidents. She believes the experience of being under the influence of the Holy Spirit for an extended period of time was essential to her healing. The outcome was both concentrated and progressive healing. The memory of sexual abuse remained but the pain was gone. She maintains that only God can do that. Her difficulty with sex was over, and she was empowered to approach further life experiences. She likens the healing to a butterfly emerging from a cocoon in that timing is crucial. Chloe believes the depth and extent of healing experiences can vary.

The Spirit and Christ

Julian

Julian understands the Spirit enabled him to receive forgiveness and acceptance through Christ. The Spirit helped him place his confidence in Christ's work as the basis of his security and significance. He believes that God understands the reality and damage of sin and, through Christ, made a full provision for his renewal and restoration. The Spirit is the trusted guide who led Julian, never pushing, to understand what God had done for him. Knowing Christ means knowing the way forward in spite of anxieties. The Spirit presents Christ moment-by-moment in everyday life and enables Julian to experience the benefits of Christ's work. The Spirit, in revealing Christ, brings security and the ability to respond out of that, authentically. In the revealing of Christ, there is a corresponding revealing of self. Julian understands the Spirit to unite the ways and will of Christ to him inwardly, in deeply personal and specific ways. What the Spirit is inwardly changing, and producing in him, is already seen in Christ. Christ is the ultimate to which the Spirit is leading, directing, and transforming people.

Summary

All forty-one interpretive themes have now been addressed in chapters 4 through 8. In this chapter, I have discussed the recovered victims' various experiences of the Holy Spirit and, in particular, the Spirit's working to bring them healing from the devastating effects of childhood sexual abuse. I will now discuss three meta-themes arising from that: the actualizing of new life capacities as the Spirit; the confidence and courage for change as the Spirit; and the movement toward shared life as the Spirit.

The Actualizing of New Life Capacities as the Spirit

Throughout Scripture, the Spirit is associated with life. The Nicene Creed calls the Spirit, "The Lord, the Giver of Life." This designation as life-giver reflects much of the biblical understanding of the Spirit's activity. In both the Old and New Testaments, the life of the Spirit is linked to creation itself, to humanity, to nature and history in general, and to the history of salvation. Dresser says the Spirit is

> the central life, the inmost activity which goes forth from the Godhead, the world-will which manifests the divine purpose . . . [and is] . . . known through what it accomplishes.[1]

It is "the power and efficacy of divine action"[2] at work, from creation to the eschatological consummation, in the dynamic process of the world and history. As such, the Spirit is "the divine ground of the evocation of all life in general," and "the gracious presence that engenders particular experiences of transformed life."[3] The Spirit is "the unceasing animator and communicator, the inexhaustible source of insight, awareness, recognition and response."[4] The presence and the activity of the Spirit is "public,"

---

1. Dresser, *Philosophy of Spirit*, 39, 41.
2. Shults and Hollingsworth, *Holy Spirit*, 49.
3. Shults and Hollingsworth, *Holy Spirit*, 3.
4. Taylor, *A Matter of Life*, 10.

"something to be recognized and experienced . . . as directly as everyday life itself."[5]

This Spirit that "moves over . . . the waters"[6] of a formless void "expresses God's vitality, God's readiness to speak and to act . . . from eternity."[7] When God "breathed . . . the breath of life" into human beings, he gave "fleshly, perishable, finite creatures a share in God's breath and thus in God's Spirit."[8] Throughout the Old Testament, there continues this great life-giving work with individuals and with the people of God. The Spirit of the Lord, *ruach-Jahweh*, enlivened and vitalized judges, kings, prophets, and other deliverers. These Old Testament fillings of the Spirit can be understood as,

> the *expansion* of the Spirit of life given to all human beings from the time of Adam (Gen 2:7) and even present in some sense in all flesh or creaturely life.[9]

In the New Testament, this life-giving aspect of the Holy Spirit is further understood in the context of the regeneration of the believer in Christ. The Spirit works ceaselessly on a spectrum from ordinary to extraordinary ways to make Christ known, to persuade human beings to trust and open themselves up to his love, and to appropriate their eschatological identity as children of God. Bloesch says,

> The Spirit of God has various roles and it is a mistake to magnify one of these over all the others. The Spirit is active in creation . . . He is at work in revelation . . . He is the principal agent in our regeneration . . . He preserves the people of God . . . He convicts people of their sins . . . He empowers the people of God.[10]

Pinnock views the Spirit

> as the bond of love in the triune relationality, as the ecstasy of sheer life overflowing into a significant creation, as the power of creation and new creation, as the power of incarnation and atonement, as

---

5. Engelbrecht, "The Indwelling," 24.
6. Gen 1:2 (NASB).
7. Welker, *God the Spirit*, 161.
8. Welker, *God the Spirit*, 159.
9. This is found in Macchia's review of John R. Levison's book, *Filled with the Spirit*, where he appreciatively explores Levinson's understanding of the gap between Old and New Testament pneumatologies.
10. Bloesch, *The Holy Spirit*, 73.

the power of new community and union with God, and as the power drawing the whole world into the truth of Jesus.[11]

The picture of Israel reaching the end of their resources as a nation in Ezekiel 3, and requiring a supernatural endowment of new life from God, is "a commentary on a constant state of affairs."[12] As such, "the Spirit is present in that which is *held together* and *enlivened* by God . . . [and] not . . . in that which is decaying to dust."[13] Just as humankind had come alive by the Spirit of God, it "continue[d] to require the Spirit as an on-going gift."[14] There is a longing in the Old Testament for a "corporate bestowal of the life of the Spirit on the whole people of God,"[15] and there is a reaching out for "the gift of immortality that comes through Christ."[16] In other words, "the flourishing of natural human life in the Old Testament . . . seems to require a solution that is not potentially available from birth . . . [but] . . . only Christ can give."[17]

In the New Testament, the Spirit proceeding from Christ's resurrection initiates "the beginning of the new creation of everything . . . a completely new life," which is a "life against death."[18] The Pentecost event touches and affects specific people in their specific situations in such a way that, "the knowledge of God and the reality intended by God are made accessible" to each and all, through "the message of faith."[19] Finite human life is taken into the divine life which is eternal. The human experience of God is an immense liberation into true life springing from a divine source which defies that which is dead and threatening. Moltmann says,

> In the experience of the Spirit, the spring of life begins to flow in us again. We begin to flower and become fruitful. An undreamt-of-love for life awakens in us, driving out the bacillus of resignation, and healing painful remembrances. We go to meet life expecting the rebirth of everything that lives, and with this expectation, we

---

11. Pinnock, *Flame of Love*, 10.
12. Macchia, "Spirit of Life," 74.
13. Welker, *God the Spirit*, 161.
14. Macchia, "Spirit of Life," 74.
15. Winn, "Holy Spirit," 48.
16. Macchia, "Spirit of Life," 74.
17. Macchia, "Spirit of Life," 75.
18. Moltmann, *Source of Life*, 30, 98.
19. Such as sickness, demonic bondage, sinfulness, powerlessness, separation, isolation, ignorance, success, culture, language, and background.

experience our own rebirth, and the rebirth we share with everything else.[20]

For Rahner, the Spirit of God is not "extrinsic" to the human person, but is "the innermost constitutive principle of human existence,"[21] "a deep, primal dynamism of transcendent love that is both the horizon and the heart of ordinary human life."[22] Faith is "an open acceptance of the deep human openness to God."[23] The experience of God fulfills a "longing to surrender," which is both a "quality of liberation" and an "expansion of self."[24] Dresser says, "strictly speaking, what is perceived is an experience too wealthy to be described."[25] Parlow says, "this mystery cannot be directly grasped by human reason but must be found in surrender."[26] Moltmann says people seek God because God draws them, and these are the first human experiences of the Spirit.[27] In their search for life and happiness, people "feel the inward tug of God's love."[28] The human experience of the Spirit prepares the way for thought. The Spirit makes God personal to the human soul in "an ineffable union," "an ineffable nearness . . . which may only be appreciatively interpreted."[29] The fresh convictions which arise are "a united product" of the Spirit and of the human person.

The participants describe the divine agency in their lives in terms of God's presentation of, and their sensibility to, new insights, perspectives, emotions, inclinations, understandings, and convictions in the heart and mind, coming either immediately or developing over time, and having the creative potential to transform the familiar into the new by calling them into freedom, new life, and wholeness.

The participants use various expressions to denote the Spirit's activity in their lives. Scarlett refers to the Spirit in relation to herself, as "prompting," "quickening," "urging," "bringing to mind," "saying," "telling," "guiding," "showing," and "filling." She indicates that these first happened in herself,

---

20. Welker, *God the Spirit*, 241, 243.
21. Rahner, *Foundations of Christian Faith*, 118.
22. Parlow, "Personal Transformation," 573.
23. Parlow, "Personal Transformation," 573.
24. Ghent, "Masochism, Submission, Surrender," 108.
25. Dresser, *Philosophy of Spirit*, 171.
26. Parlow, "Personal Transformation," 574.
27. Moltmann, *Spirit of Life*, 93.
28. Moltmann, *Spirit of Life*, 94.
29. Moltmann, *Spirit of Life*, 172.

The Holy Spirit

in her spirit, and were, from there, worked out with her cooperation. She refers to herself in relation to the Spirit as "experiencing," "sensing," "becoming aware," being "unaware," being "born again," "learning," "becoming more alive," and "growing."

Sometimes the Spirit's work was experienced with immediacy, and is described as "a sudden flash," "dropping into" or "putting a finger on" an issue. At other times, the Spirit's work was experienced "more gradually," and "slowly over time." Reflection on difficult circumstances that she had passed through, indicated that the Spirit had been doing some work there as well.

The outcome of these experiences was that she was enabled to step up to another level with God. She understands that, through her life, the Holy Spirit was teaching her about God, the Father, loving her and wanting the best for her so she could learn to trust him in preparation for that time when he could start to rebuild her life. Scarlett indicated that her experience of God was always an experience of love. The Holy Spirit taught her that God is always love and always trustworthy.

Liam refers to the Spirit in relation to himself as "revealing" and "leading." He refers to himself as "feeling," "knowing," "picking up," and "having a picture." He indicates that he was surprised by how accurate his pastoral counselors were in praying through issues with him. He found things coming up which he wasn't expecting. He attributes their hitting the nail on the head to being willing to be led by the Spirit. This was comforting, encouraging, and indicative of God's ongoing plan for his life.

Chloe maintains that, as a child, she had a "drive to love" that was "a God thing," but really never understood the love of God. She understands that from conversion, the Holy Spirit lived inside her. Chloe refers to the Spirit in relation to herself as "speaking to her heart," "dealing with her," "doing surgery," "showing," "leading," "guiding," "telling," "helping, "restoring," "healing," and "releasing." She refers to herself in relation to the Spirit, as being "open to be loved again," "loving others, "glowing, "remembering," "realizing," "trusting," "thinking," "surrendering," "laughing," and "being in his presence."

Julian refers to spiritual experiences where something happened which he didn't fully understand. When words came to him, he felt he had to surrender something but didn't know why. He describes these experiences as God helping him. In reflecting upon and trying to describe how the Spirit operates, he wonders, "Is it the Spirit who helps me see differently?"

He understands himself to have reached points in his life where he doesn't have the answer anymore and has to stop and listen and learn something new. He describes it as stepping out of what he already knew and stepping into the unknown, giving rise to a new perception. He says, "All of a sudden I can see it for what it is . . . and I'm empowered to do something." He understands coming to see properly is the Holy Spirit working who wants him to know the truth, and the lie as well. These "invitations from the Spirit" for help have always been there.

He maintains that the work of the Spirit in relation to himself is really revealing, including revealing himself, his forgiveness, and his ability to forgive. He further speaks of the Spirit "empowering," "speaking," "guiding," "allowing," "comforting," and "healing." In contrast to previous inabilities, he refers to himself in relation to the Spirit as "seeing," "listening," "hearing," "feeling," "sensing," "knowing," and "trusting."

Sophia describes the human spirit as a candle which is ignited at salvation, through an indwelling of the Spirit of Christ, miraculously given by God. For her, this flame began as a flicker when she was a child and later increased, when through teaching she experienced a Holy Spirit awakening, and "lights started going on." She refers to the Spirit in relation to her spiritual and healing journeys, as "indwelling," "awakening," "prompting," "saying," "showing," "challenging," "renewing, "healing," and "restoring." She refers to herself in relation to the Spirit, as "realizing," "seeing," "knowing," "believing," "hearing," "feeling," and "interceding."

Emma understands her teenage decision to receive Christ was something that helped her. She understood that she didn't have to be a victim. She describes her adult conversion as a time when God came out of nowhere into her life, resulting in her kneeling, praying and surrendering, even though she didn't understand it. In this coming, the Spirit gave her a new life. Emma refers to the Spirit in relation to herself as a voice which came to her as God who kept coming into her life, as God working in her life, and as God redirecting her life. This voice has been described by Emma as "speaking," "convincing," "showing," "intervening," "instilling," and "healing." The Spirit has gently dealt with her life, picked her up, taken her through, and made brokenness into something beautiful.

Emma understands that the Holy Spirit comes in this way when you are ready, because "he really knows what you are going through," "what needs to be changed," what's important, and knows what you don't. The key for Emma was having her identity in God. It was the Holy Spirit who taught her to start believing God's perceptions rather than her own. Emma refers to herself in relation to Spirit, as "I knew," "I was convinced," "I realized," "I opened myself up to be directed," "I learned to walk in the Spirit," "I learned to listen to God," "just allowing God," and "suddenly seeing the truth."

Adam distinguishes between knowing about the Holy Spirit as a young person, and the experience of being baptized in the Holy Spirit. Something happened and all the things he knew about Jesus were made alive by the Holy Spirit. The Jesus he knew was not fulfilled in him until he had the Holy Spirit, when it all began to come alive and Adam was full of joy. He refers to the Spirit in relation to himself as "a spark lit by Christ" which gave a sense of God with him and in him. For Adam, understanding the work of the Spirit was what conversion was all about. For him, it is the Spirit who makes alive and "stirs our inner soul." Adam describes this new life as a complete change where he didn't smoke or drink anymore, read the Bible more, and had love for everybody.

The Impetus, Confidence, and Courage for Change as the Spirit

The Spirit proceeds from the cross and resurrection of Jesus as the quickening and activating power, actualizing the creation of something totally new within this world: a new life, a new person, a new society.

For Barth, this work of the Spirit is "pre-eminently in the perception and recognition [of] that which has already, objectively and *de jure*, been accomplished in Christ for all human beings."[30] The Spirit, as the human experience of the presence of God, is the personal beginning of new life, described as rebirth and regeneration and the possibility of ongoing progressive activity and realization, described as sanctification or *theosis*. Pentecost is the Spirit of God, as the Spirit of the resurrection of the dead, himself invading the world, redeeming and sanctifying it, to the end of consummating the renewal of all things.

The regenerate person "is ahead of . . . [themselves], as it were . . . [living] from what is coming to meet . . . [them], not from what already exists in . . . [them]" but looking towards God's future.[31] There is a dynamic tension between the present and the eschaton and "the Holy Spirit is this

---

30. Moltmann, *Spirit of Life*, 150–51.
31. Moltmann, *Spirit of Life*, 151.

tension personified."[32] Regeneration means a personal beginning of new life living in hope. The infinite God is present as the breath of life of the new world, in the human experiences of newfound peace with God, the joy of new life, and the possession of hope, making these experiences not only of "unfathomable depth," but of "unlimited potentialities."[33]

The Spirit, who is the life-giver, is also the "power to form" that same life. Dresser says, "God is essentially dynamic, achieving; it is life, movement, growth, that reveals him."[34] It is this "moving or quickening power . . . that ever sends us forward in pursuit of the perfect."[35] Welker says that human beings,

> are given a part in the movement from God to God . . . in the permanent process of becoming, both distinct from God and related to God . . . becoming *ever more human* or more precisely, *peculiarly human*.[36]

The Holy Spirit, then, is "a battling, conquering Spirit" struggling relentlessly against all that is dehumanizing and deprives God's children of their true identity and destiny. Engelbrecht says, "as the power of change, he starts precisely where the prospects of change seem to be faintest."[37]

Moltmann maintains that "the transcendent depth" and "the eschatological breath" of the Spirit means *rebirth* or *regeneration* cannot be a once-and-for-all experience, or something finished and past. He says those who have received the Spirit "are still involved in the experience of renewal" and "the becoming-new travels with us."[38] He maintains that "a Christian's being is in becoming . . . [This] becoming is a continual repentance, a continual start in a new direction."[39] And again, "if the primal experience of the Spirit is called *rebirth*, this metaphor implies *growth* in faith, in knowledge and wisdom.[40] With reference to Wesley's understanding of sin as sickness, Moltmann says,

---

32. Engelbrecht, "The Indwelling," 29.
33. Moltmann, *Spirit of Life*, 155.
34. Dresser, *Philosophy of Spirit*, 4.
35. Dresser, *Philosophy of Spirit*, 34.
36. Welker, *God the Spirit*, 45.
37. Engelbrecht, "The Indwelling," 31.
38. Moltmann, *Spirit of Life*, 155.
39. Moltmann, *Experiences of God*, 4.
40. Moltmann, *Spirit of Life*, 161.

If sanctification is really the healing of the spiritual life in men and women, then it must also be possible to detect the stages of returning health. Like a sick person, the sinner can also contribute to the process of recovering . . . [their] spiritual health. Of course, everything is always dependent upon God's grace, but this grace also lays hold of the sinful will and liberates it, awakening new energies in it.[41]

In relation to the human response to *new life*, Loder says,

Just as Adam, formed and *in-breathed* with the breath of life (Gen. 2:7), was given a task to perform (Gen 2:18), so . . . once the human spirit is awakened to its origin and true ground, it must exercise the freedom inherent in being spirit and choose to respond and conform to the in-breathing of the life of God.[42]

In that *new and incorruptible life* begins a new history within the old, involving the "defatalization of . . . [the] world,"[43] and, human-wise, the bringing forth of a new being who is remembering the things that Jesus taught about humans, sins, redemption, and glory. This new being is being guided by "a love that is unfailing, a wisdom that encompasses every need."[44] They live in anticipation, expectation, and the gradual realization of God's future through the Spirit.

Williams finds an understanding of the Holy Spirit as "the engine" in Anselm's theology, which brings about the teleological fulfillment of both the Godhead and humankind. The Spirit provides a *teleological impetus* within the Trinity, which is present also in human redemption and sanctification. In the Godhead, the Holy Spirit "serves as the perfect love by which the self-contained and static divine wisdom is made dynamic and purposeful."[45] The same dynamism works in human lives when that same love is poured into human hearts. Williams says,

---

41. Moltmann, *Spirit of Life*, 164.
42. Loder, *Logic of Spirit*, 112.
43. Engelbrecht, "The Indwelling," 31.
44. Welker, *God the Spirit*, 131.
45. Williams, "God Who Sows the Seed," 627. Williams points out that Anselm avoids the idea that the Father and Son would be useless without the Spirit with a "robust doctrine of *perichoresis*, whereby, each of the three persons is individually essentially memory and understanding and love, so that none of the persons needs another in order to remember, understand or love," 615.

in the spiritual life, the Holy Spirit energizes and makes fruitful the human nature that the Father has created and the Son has redeemed so that rational creatures achieve their appointed end.[46]

The Holy Spirit gives life to human beings beyond the capacity of their nature. Williams cites Anselm's meditation in First Corinthians 3:9, entitled "You are God's husbandry," as a description of this process of fecundity and growth:

> Consider how the earth, without any effort on our part, brings forth countless plants and trees that do nothing to nourish human nature, or even kill us, whereas those that are most necessary to sustain our lives require tremendous effort and someone to cultivate them, and they do not grow without seeds. In the same way, human hearts require no teaching or effort in order to sprout, effortlessly, thoughts and wills that are in no way useful for salvation or are actually harmful; but it is only through seeds of the proper sort and with diligent cultivation that they conceive and produce the thoughts and wills without which we do not make progress toward the souls salvation. This is why the Apostle calls those who benefit from this work of cultivation "Gods husbandry."[47]

For Anselm, the "seeds of the proper sort," planted by the Holy Spirit, are both understandings given from Scripture and given directly to a person. The Spirit is then both the "sower" and "cultivator" of these "supernatural" seed. He not only plants the seeds of right understanding but also cultivates "the seed of right action."[48]

Interpreting Paul's concept of the Spirit in Galatians, Lull maintains the Spirit effects more than "a change in one's perception of reality"; it brings "a new structure of existence."[49] *Pneumatic ecstasy*, as the prerequisite for doing God's will, together with the "genuinely historical" and dynamic nature of human existence means the believer is no longer enslaved, but has an alternative orientation and the freedom to choose the "goals and intentions of the Spirit" over the "goals and intentions" of the flesh (Gal 5:13b, 16–17; Rom 8:5–7, 27).[50] Human effort participates in the restructuring of the

---

46. Williams, "God Who Sows the Seed," 611.

47. Williams, "God Who Sows the Seed," 616. Found in *De cordial* 3.6 (II.270, 380–81).

48. Williams, "God Who Sows the Seed," 618.

49. Lull, "The Spirit," 45.

50. By which Lull means, "the incursion of the divine Spirit in the *heart* of the

The Holy Spirit

human self, through choices made in accordance with the will of the Spirit, so maintaining a life in the Spirit which empowers transformation. Growth in the spiritual life is not automatic, and the Spirit's role in the process is "persuasive" rather than "coercive." Humphrey says,

> Any health, any growth we experience comes from him, whether we are aware of this or not: but the conscious cultivation of the life that God has in mind for us is connected to our full celebration and concentration upon this mystery of God's ecstasy and intimacy, portrayed in Jesus the Christ.[51]

Rahner coined the term *supernatural existential*, to designate the orientation of human beings to a supernatural end. Parlow explains this to mean that

> human beings are more than creatures of time and space alone ... we are, at root, open to universal presence, limitless Being—a dizzying incomprehensibility that the passion of faith assures us is beneficent.[52]

Cross maintains that as finite human persons "we are given the capacity by the grace of God," to "experience infinite love and even the presence of the Infinite One."[53] Encountering God's presence results in "a radical openness to God's presence and power"[54] as one learns for oneself who God really is. God graciously offers the resources of God's own self—"peace, joy, the experience of being loved, and strength to do improbable good"—so life can be approached "in hope, trust and love" and "higher possibilities."[55] Experiencing God's presence in the Spirit "opens up a different basis of expectation" and means a person "confidently expect[s] a graced future that is not the outcome of mere human foresight and planning but exceeds it."[56]

This hope is based on God's call to the divine life. This is not without struggle and with reference to "the certainty within the uncertainty of the struggle," Moltmann says,

---

believer." Lull, "The Spirit," 43.
51. Humphrey, *Ecstasy and Intimacy*, 5.
52. Parlow, "Personal Transformation," 577.
53. Cross, "The Divine-Human Encounter," 18.
54. Cross, "The Divine-Human Encounter," 6.
55. Parlow, "Personal Transformation," 576–77.
56. Parlow, "Personal Transformation," 576–77.

> The favorite and much quoted text, 'It does *not yet appear* what we shall be' is ... preceded with a declaration of confidence: 'Beloved, we are God's children *now*.' It is this trust, after all, which spurs hope on; and it is this very *being* of God's children which is in the process of *becoming* in the Christian's life and death."[57]

Learning to hope in the experiences of life, knowing that in everything God is working "for good for those who love him and are called according to his purpose" (Rom 8:28), brings inner security into the struggle. The inner peace that God's Spirit brings is not *repose*, but "a tumultuous activity within as the courage of the person is mobilized for ... the growth of a new self under God."[58] Faith is

> the affirmation of the work of God through the acceptance of that inner struggle of the soul and the response of the whole person to become the person which God in both his creation and redemption intends that one be ... involves the tearing up of old securities ... the courage of not knowing, but responding to the call of God to a new life. It is not shrinking back from the demands of growth and maturity. It is moving out beyond the safe confines of a known way.[59]

Beck refers to Tavard's designation of the Spirit as both *Consoler* and *Achiever* to account for the Spirit's agency in transformation toward Christlikeness. He says,

> As Consoler, the Spirit comes to us; allowing us to participate in the gift and the infusion of grace and granting us hope that the journey will reach its *telos* in union with God. As Achiever, the Spirit brings the soul to perfection, completely sanctifying it, inevitably by means of suffering.[60]

He refers to Mark 1:12, John of the Cross, and Gregory of Nyssa to convey the idea of the *dis-comforting* effect of the Spirit for the greater purpose. Mark tells us the Spirit *drove* Jesus into the wilderness to struggle with the Tempter. The word *ekballo* denotes "a forceful action." *The ascent of Mt. Carmel* and *Life of Moses* use the image of a mountain to depict the spiritual journey. Beck maintains,

---

57. Moltmann, *Experiences of God*, 5.
58. Oates, "Holy Spirit as Counsellor," 239.
59. Oates, "Holy Spirit as Counsellor," 239.
60. Beck, "The Divine Dis-Comforter," 207.

The Holy Spirit

> There are no ski lifts on the mountain of God . . . The Holy Spirit acts as divine agent in . . . summoning, enabling, and demanding that the soul travel this one-and-only path to union with God.[61]

The seven recovered victims' narratives disclose both the *comforting and enabling* aspects of the Spirit's work. There is both the *confidence* for change and growth, and the more *persuasive and challenging* aspects of the Spirit's work, requiring *courage* to continue to move forward and change. The confidence and courage for change, which were at times mixed with other feelings, were attributed to the Spirit.

For Scarlett, the impetus to seek pastoral counseling, and the confidence and courage to complete the process of healing, came from the Spirit. The Spirit told her to start, directed her to the pastoral counselor, and guided the sessions. Scarlett's confidence came from her experience of God, enabling her to trust him enough and "knowing that God was directing every part of it." She describes herself as having "come to that place where when the Holy Spirit said something I obeyed and did it." Walking with God and obeying God, in the sense of personally communing with him through the Spirit as distinct from following what she'd been told, was fundamental to her growth.

For her, the Spirit sometimes conveyed thoughts with an urgency. Over time, she learned that she should listen to those thoughts and obey, because the Spirit speaking meant it was important. Scarlett found this to be costly, but knew, in the end, "there would be blessing in it." Through all of this, "God was building character."

Sophia and Chloe each experienced being overwhelmed by the Spirit, repeatedly, over a period of time. While their encounters are personal, there are similarities with regard to the impetus it provided, and the confidence resulting for ongoing change. For Chloe, the encounter brought insight, initiated healing, and led to subsequent growth. Experiencing the "tangible presence" of God meant she knew he was with her and didn't leave her even through the abuse. She has maintained that conviction ever since.[62]

For Sophia, experiencing the overwhelming presence of God over time "built . . . [her] faith that God would actually move without an atmosphere being created, [and] without other people being around . . . [her]." While she lists many things that have contributed to her spiritual growth,

---

61. Beck, "The Divine Dis-Comforter," 208.

62. This is why Chloe felt she could participate in these interviews without her husband present.

when she reached a point of saying, "I like who I am; I don't want to grow anymore," it was the Holy Spirit who responded, "Nah, we're moving on." She also understands that the Holy Spirit guided her to Christian resources which gradually helped renew her mind.

When Liam was convinced that his pastoral counselors were picking things up through the Spirit with accuracy, he found it really comforting, and was prepared to revisit previously dealt with issues at a deeper level. While he wanted everything dealt with now, and everything fixed, he sees that the timing was right. He sees that God used time between healings as training. He understands it as a progressive journey where God has been shaping him. He learned that "when God is ready to do something, he will deal with it." He feels there may be more things that come up over time, but it's up to God.

Julian refers to the Holy Spirit as the comforter, or a safe place where the truth was exposed. He was able to actually see things for what they were, express himself, and not have to fix anything because Jesus embraced the sin and fixed it—he finished the work. While the abuse has affected who Julian is, the Spirit says, "This is who you [really] are, and I'm going to help you." Julian feels he can trust the presence, but nowhere else is safe. The work of the Spirit was to reveal Christ in a true sense as "I'm forgiven" and provide the ability for Julian to listen to and trust that. He understands that "there is a process of bringing it to the cross," which means it has to resurface, and the Spirit is really engaging in being around it and surrounding it. Julian understands that it is through the Spirit that he was able to experience more of God's love.

Emma could only believe God's perception—the right perspective—about herself because the Holy Spirit continued teaching her. She could be thinking one way and the Spirit would change her mind. The Spirit taught her to see what was wrong in her life, things she might've not noticed, such as unforgiveness. The Spirit helped her find her identity in God and helped her really understand the father heart of God. The Spirit helped her stop justifying herself and judging others. Emma doesn't believe she would have been able to look herself like that without the Spirit of God. Only the Holy Spirit knows what needs to be changed. Only the Spirit helped her really understand that God was not judging her all the time, and that God loved her so much.

The Spirit made both sudden and gradual changes in Adam's life. After being baptized in the Spirit, he stopped drinking and smoking and the

Spirit grew in him. He had a real sense of joy, which he had never known, and a new desire to read the Bible and pray. His whole life opened up—his mind bloomed and his heart blossomed. It was the Spirit who changed everything. Adam learned to forgive, which he believes is due to the Holy Spirit. He had such a sense of God that nothing mattered except him. He could address issues because God was with him and in him. He was compelled by the Spirit to sort things out. Since he knew the Holy Spirit was with him, he knew, with confidence, that there was an end. Adam says, "The Holy Spirit made me very strong on some things." He could be a bit bolder, more loving, and more persuasive because he wasn't frightened. The Holy Spirit gave him confidence that he did not normally have.

The Movement Toward Shared Life as the Spirit

Persons, having been created in the image of God, know their personhood through relation to others. Marshall says, "Our identity is established by communing with others, even as the divine persons draw identity through perichoretic movement."[63] The eighth-century notion of perichoresis has been described as "an eternal reciprocity of energy within God by virtue of the divine love."[64] As such, community is the "appropriate metaphor for God"—"a relationality that celebrates diversity in unity."[65]

Within the depths of the divine reality, "unity is everlastingly generated from a fundamental diversity," and "diversity, is everlastingly generated from a fundamental unity."[66] Zizioulas says, it is because the ground of God's ontological freedom lies in his personal "mode of [Trinitarian] existence" that human persons, created in his image, can have "hope of becoming authentic persons."[67] In communion with God, they are transformed into a new mode of existence, "an ecclesial hypostasis." Thus, "what is valid for God" is also "valid for man" by a progressive movement of transformed levels of being.

Paul connects the experience of the Holy Spirit, who actualizes this communion, to the formation and flourishing of community which he calls *the body of Christ*. The body of Christ, according to Barth is "not a mass of

---

63. Marshall, *Joining the Dance*, 101.
64. Suchocki, "Theological Foundations," 39.
65. Suchocki, "Theological Foundations," 39, 41.
66. Suchocki, "Theological Foundations," 40.
67. Zizioulas, *Being as Communion*, 44, 48.

individuals, not even a corporation, a personified society, or a 'totality,' but The Individual, The One, The New."[68]

Just as the divine Trinitarian relations are sustained by "God's openness to otherness,"[69] so believers "are called to an existence with *perforated boundaries*."[70] Marshall describes this openness as "a willingness to experience oneself as unfinished."[71] This openness and mutuality of relation mean an increasing enrichment of experience, affecting both a transcendence and transformation of the self. Suchocki describes this in terms of "a change of being," where "sensuous existence," characterized by "a self or tribal centeredness," is replaced by "spiritual existence," characterized by "an outward movement toward embracing otherness in love."[72]

The Spirit, who unites persons, divine, and human, begins the believer's life in Christ and joins them to the people of God. LaCugna refers to "the proper work of the Spirit," as "the achievement of communion." She says,

> The Spirit gathers together in Christ persons who would not otherwise gather, making possible a true union of hearts and minds, the ground of which resides not in individual differences—age, gender, opinions, abilities—but in the very being of God. The Spirit accomplishes unity-amidst-diversity, a communion that abolishes solitariness but not individuality.[73]

The divine presence is identified in the gathering, forming and sustaining of individuals into a community where Christ is made present. With reference to Joel's prophecy (Joel 2:28–32), quoted by Peter as fulfilled on the day of Pentecost, Welker says,

> When the Spirit of God is poured out, the different persons and groups of people will open God's presence with each other and for each other. With each other and for each other, they will make it possible to know the reality intended by God. They will enrich and strengthen each other and for each other, they will make it possible to know the reality intended by God. They will enrich and strengthen each other through their differentiated prophetic

---

68. Barth, *Epistle to Romans*, 443.
69. Marshall, *Joining the Dance*, 108.
70. Suchocki, "Theological Foundations," 43.
71. Marshall, *Joining the Dance*, 108.
72. Suchocki, "Theological Foundations," 402.
73. La Cugna, *God for Us*, 298.

knowledge. From various perspectives and trajectories of experience, they will direct each other's attention to the agent responsible for their deliverance. But in this differentiated community of testimony, not only is there a powerful continuation of the Spirit's working toward righteousness. In this differentiated and pluriform community of testimony, God becomes present in a concentrated way. What is striking is the only apparently paradoxical state of affairs that is precisely in the differentiated abundance of prophetic attestation that God wills to make Godself knowable in a powerful and concentrated way.[74]

The Spirit works to sustain the *perichoresis* of the various members of the one body of Christ. Each member of this heterogeneous gathering is to value the diversity of charisms and submit themselves to the unifying work of the Spirit. Sarot argues that "being the body of Christ is given to the Christian community not as a possession but as a task to fulfill through the power of the Spirit."[75] God's relationship with humanity, is not primarily one between two individuals but between "a community and a Trinity: a triune God."[76] Jesus said to Saul in Acts (9:4; 22:7; 26:14), "Why do you persecute me?," indicating the incorporation of the church into Christ. Zizioulas says the Holy Spirit

> actually realizes in history that which we call Christ . . . This application of Christ's existence to ours then amounts to nothing other than a realization of the community of the Church. This community is born as the Body of Christ and lives out of the same communion which we find in Christ's historical existence. His *true life* is identical with the eternal life of the Triune God.[77]

The church as the body of Christ is participating in the relationship between the Father and the Son through the Spirit and, as such, in the *missio Dei*. The missions of God in the world are firstly processions within God's eternal being.[78] God comes from God in the person of the Father; to Himself in the world, the Son; and as God, the Holy Spirit. So as Fiddes says, "there is no other God than the one who is open to others in outward-going love, and the God who makes communion in the world must already

---

74. Welker, *God the Spirit*, 151.
75. Sarot, "Trinity and Church," 33.
76. Sarot, "Trinity and Church," 33.
77. Zizioulas, *Being as Communion*, 110, 111, 114.
78. Fiddes, *Participating in God*, 170.

be in communion."⁷⁹ Incorporation by the Spirit into the sonship of Christ is then "necessarily communal . . . for the Spirit brings together humanity into the unity of Christ."⁸⁰

Life in the Spirit will always push toward communal experience. The coming together of the early church on the first day of the week, as individuals resurrected into community, was "driven by the wind of the Spirit."⁸¹ The Spirit fell on them "all together in one place," resulting in new and shared life in community (Acts 2). Brunner says,

> The Body of Christ is nothing other than a fellowship of persons. It is "the fellowship of Jesus Christ" or "fellowship of the Holy Ghost" where fellowship or koinonia signifies a common participation, a togetherness, a community life. The faithful are bound to each other through their common sharing in Christ and in the Holy Ghost, but that which they have in common is no "thing," no "it," but a "he," Christ and his Holy Spirit.⁸²

Kainen calls this "a fellowship of charismatics," where "the life of the community is participatory," and *charismata* establish an interdependence, "a fellowship of mutual giving and receiving."⁸³ This organic expression of resurrection life means "[these] communities empowered by the Spirit . . . [become] places of healing and transformation."⁸⁴

The Spirit works to form communities of people who are open to God, one another, and God's future and, are in partnership with God's mission of "world transformation,"⁸⁵ and, the summing up all things in Christ. To this end the Spirit goes ahead of the church, preparing the hearts of people for the coming of the church.⁸⁶ The church follows after "to make open and visible what the Spirit has already begun in secret."⁸⁷

The Spirit is pre-eminently characterized by movement. Welker says, "the Spirit is the power that moves the people of God."⁸⁸ Faith means

---

79. Fiddes, *Participating in God*, 6.
80. Dodds, "The Mission," 211–12.
81. Marshall, *Joining the Dance*, 90.
82. Brunner, *Misunderstanding of Church*, 10–11.
83. Kainen, *Toward a Pneumatological Theology*, 119–20.
84. Kainen, "Spirit, Reconciliation and Healing," 46.
85. Dodds, "The Mission," 209.
86. Newbigin, *Trinitarian Doctrine*, 40.
87. Welker, *God the Spirit*, 213.
88. Welker, *God the Spirit*, 14.

responding to God's call to a new life, and entails "moving out beyond the confines of a safe way," moving out of loneliness, isolation, overcoming anxiety, and moving into "the reality of communion in the family of God" where there is progressive movement out toward others and toward God-likeness.[89] Marshall says,

> "Spirit is always moving ahead, drawing . . . to new life and receptivity to God's presence with us . . . [and] gather[ing] a people to be a particular expression of God's presence in the world . . . the formation of a community that . . . function[s] as God's own . . . a uniting community characterized by fellowship and ecstasy."[90]

This movement, into the shared life of this community, is the Spirit "in perichoretic dance, drawing . . . into the movement of the divine life of God."[91]

All the participants refer to the work of the Spirit in terms of movement. Their transcripts reveal movements towards openness with others, relational depth, and church involvement as the drawing movement of the Spirit. That significant obstacles and barriers often needed to be traversed and overcome highlights the work of the Spirit, which is the power to cross barriers.

Scarlett, Liam, and Chloe have attended church all their lives and are presently involved in ministry and, yet, their abuse came from within the church. Scarlett's father took the family to church and, yet, he was her perpetrator. Liam is now a pastor and his perpetrator was his father and pastor. He experienced negative reactions, even hostility, from members of the congregation when the perpetrator was exposed. Chloe grew up in a church community and was abused by an elder of her church. Nonetheless, all have continued to attend church, make progress in their spiritual journey, become involved in ministry, and find their healing through the church community.

When Scarlett decided to "make a public stand for God," she discovered and was drawn to other girls in the class that were also Christians and going to church. They started attending youth group together. Perceiving a spiritual depth in a certain person, she was drawn to hanging out with her. She describes connecting to people like that as a God thing, because she felt she could talk to them and, potentially, relate deeply with them. Reference

89. Oates, "Holy Spirit as Counsellor," 239, 241.
90. Marshall, *Joining the Dance*, 3, 4, 37, 38, 77.
91. Marshall, *Joining the Dance*, 114.

to the things holding her back indicates the recognition of future possibilities and a direction in which the Spirit was moving her. This movement involved openness with her pastoral counselor and other believers.

When Chloe had a personal encounter with Christ, she had to stand up, speak, and share her journey. Since then, she has felt compelled to share her healing journey with other believers. When she shared her story overseas, the service-leader interpreted it as "a God-given moment for . . . [others] to open up." Consequently, they spent two to three hours just praying for the fifty women present. Chloe was broken with the realization that women cover up the pain and only the power of God takes the pain away. Chloe believes that victims who have faced and accepted their abuse must be open to God, welcome those they can trust into their life, and be open to being loved again.

Sophia understands now that the reason she stopped attending church at seventeen was because she felt unworthy. Many years later, she realized how much influence the church had on her. She realized it had impacted her emotional growth, protection, and spiritual growth. When she became aware that she couldn't do it on her own, she knew where to go back to. This awareness and realization of the way forward is understood as the work of the Spirit. Although she has had unhelpful experiences, when she tries to share or pray with other believers, she maintains the church is the only place where God provides all that is needed to heal and become whole again. She now knows it was "more about . . . *their* spiritual journey," and that the journey isn't over.

Julian returned to a congregation after there had been a church-split because the church is about the people. He felt God say that each person is precious. When he started to engage, he could see God in people. He understands the Spirit to be "the guide we need to be able to trust . . . [and] share just that little bit." He feels it is in listening to others that we listen to ourselves. He sees that it is Christ in them that brings the transformation in him. He recalls instances where others have completely brought release to his life. This interdependence, where the Holy Spirit operates, is "a level playing field," where there are no limitations, no boundaries, and no hierarchy.

Emma's response to an encounter with God was to return to church, become progressively involved, and, after healing, enter ordained ministry. She has always wanted to hear what the Holy Spirit was saying and be directed by it. By being open, she has come to know that she belongs to God and has been born again into a new family. She has been helped through various ministries in the local and wider church where she knows the Spirit is speaking to her. She has also found that the more she encourages others, the more she gets encouraged. She believes it is by opening up to the things of God that it all starts coming in. By wanting to learn and always listening, she can say "you're right," and experience a change in perception. So, to hear the voice of God, both personally and within the context of the church community, is very important for her.

When Adam was baptized in the Holy Spirit, he felt he had to get up in church, say what happened to him, and offer prayer for the whole congregation. Previously, if there had been something negative happening in the church, he wouldn't do anything. But once he was baptized in the Holy Spirit, he felt he couldn't leave it, and the Spirit made him sort out difficulties. The Spirit caused him to be a bit more loving. He felt the Spirit drove him to get relationships right with his father and brother. He also found that he could forgive those who had abused him. At church, formality didn't matter anymore; what mattered was that they were in it together.

Conclusion

In this chapter, I have addressed the subject matter of the work of the Spirit in the lives of the seven victims who have experienced recovery from childhood sexual abuse and attribute that to the Spirit. I have explored, by means of a phenomenological analysis, the experiences of the recovered victims from which meaning for the work of the Spirit in healing can be disclosed. The participants believe themselves to be the recipients of the efficacious presence of God, which has actualized new life or vitality in them, together with new capacities issuing from that life.

Furthermore, their orientation toward, and expectation of, ongoing change for better, and the confidence and courage to overcome obstacles and move into a new future, is attributed to the Spirit. The benefits of the release from the pain and hopelessness of the past and a certain hope for a new future is grounded in the person and work of Christ and experienced by them through the Spirit. They understand that salvation in Christ means the transformation of the self, which is being progressively realized through the Spirit.

The participants further experience the working of the Spirit in the ongoing formation of their new life within the context of Christian community. They not only benefited from the diverse ministries of the Spirit within their church communities but, through dependence upon the Spirit, sought to benefit others. The Christian community was understood as the movement of the Spirit of God to consummate their revealed destiny in Christ together.

9

A MODEL FOR SPIRITUAL MINISTRY TO VICTIMS OF CHILDHOOD SEXUAL ABUSE

Introduction

IN THIS FINAL CHAPTER, we will discuss, in distilled form, those core themes which are discovered in the participants' experiences of the work of the Holy Spirit in the context of healing from childhood sexual abuse. What does the Spirit distinctively do to bring about their healing? How then should these insights into the Spirit working in healing inform and shape best ministry practice?

The Work of the Spirit in Healing

The Perspective of the Recovered Victim

Victims of childhood sexual abuse become aware, through a process of insight and reinterpretation, that they have been deceived and damaged and remain without the resources, internally and externally, to penetrate to the root issues and problems to find freedom, healing, and restoration.

Various coping mechanisms, escapes, and distractions are employed over years, but the deep wounds of the soul remain, and the pain continues, whether consciously or subconsciously.

Once the victim is moved from denial, in some way, toward disclosure and acceptance of the abuse, there comes a growing awareness that the devastation to the soul has been underestimated. There are significant debilitating effects in relation to normal functioning.

The victims find themselves in a place where the soul aches for deliverance from pain and longs to be at peace and feel itself to be free, but anxieties, mistrust, anger, shame, guilt, self-loathing, and grief continue to arise from a depth that seems impenetrable. Secular counseling, psychology, and even Christian counseling do not supply a felt sense of meaning, hope, esteem, belonging, and being loved.[1]

There is a continuing search to find that which can reach to the depths of the human spirit and impart new life. Over time, it becomes apparent that the spiritual dimension of the problem can only be addressed in personal connection with the Spirit of God. Knowing about God is insufficient to address the deep-seated wounds within the victim whose soul is in need of renewal within the context of safe, accepting, forgiving, open, supportive, and efficacious relationships.

At times, certain individuals provide a relational connection where there is a drawing toward openness. The buried conflicts within beckon to surface, find light, reality, and relief. A measure of disclosure may occur, governed by the victim's assessment of the capacity of the other, both to lovingly understand, and to offer care. Sometimes setbacks occur from the shock, distress, and disappointment of unanticipated responses.

In the healing journey, these are times of searching for, and seeking out, environments which allow for healing processes to occur. These are relational contexts with another human being, the felt presence of God, or both. That other people assist in this process, though not perfectly or completely, is indicative of both the relational nature of healing and the felt-need for relationship with someone who is completely trustworthy.

Through participation in the faith community of the church, the victim is discovering a new identity in relationship to Christ. This relationship offers both the resolution to their conflicts and hope for the future.

Their new life is understood to be progressively shaped by the presence and power of the Spirit, within the context of the body of Christ. The various ministries within the church bring a new foundation and focus for life. Various moments of insight, through the Spirit, reinforce the hope of a new and better future.

---

1. This refers to Christian counseling when it is prescriptive.

A Model for Spiritual Ministry to Victims

Every step forward in spiritual growth and healing is attributed to cooperating with God. Pastoral counseling and prayer are efficacious when the presence and leading of the Holy Spirit is experienced. It is in this environment, of trusting the person, presence, and power of the Spirit, that the victim is willingly vulnerable, honest, and transparent, and receptive to help.

Confidence in the love, knowledge, and wisdom of the Spirit leads to an openness to wounds and inner conflicts and hope in God's future. It is the Spirit who brings resolution and affects a new creation. The victim understands that union with the Spirit through Christ means change and freedom. The Spirit knows them intimately, loves them unconditionally, and works in and for them transformationally.

The confidence and courage for change and growth, which is often difficult, is enabled by the Spirit. Indeed, without the work of the Spirit in their life, the victim is without hope or the capacity for recovery. It is through the Spirit, working within the context of Christian community, that both the doors of the past and the future are opened. For the victim, these are doors that God alone can open, and once open, cannot be shut.

The Perspective of the Researcher

Those people who have experienced healing in this way are able to say in the words of the Apostles' Creed, "I believe in the Holy Spirit," not only by way of concurring with the teaching of the church, but as deep-seated, personal, healing relationship. For them, the Holy Spirit is "a truth-revealing power,"[2] through which the self undergoes transformation.

The knowing events, which have worked transformationally in the victims' lives, are the work of the Spirit who, through intimate communion and communication, brings a strong sense of a valuable and lovable self and enables epistemological integration and healing, Not only is life redefined in terms of oneself, others, God, and the world, but these are experienced and responded to differently. There is now the expectation, capacity, and courage for ongoing change through the Spirit.

---

2. Welker, *God the Spirit*, xvi.

The Work of the Spirit and Ministerial Practice

We have located ten core themes which reside within the phenomenon of the work of the Holy Spirit in bringing healing to victims of childhood sexual abuse who are Christians, and which are relevant to church life and pastoral ministry. They are as follows:

The Wounded Soul is Under Constraint to Heal

The victim's sense of self is damaged and changed by the abuse that has been suffered. However, there remains a powerful inner drive toward health and wholeness. The human self is formed through dialogical relationship in a continually changing world of experience of which the self is at the center, and, as such, is always an entity in the process of becoming. Encounter, as the beginning of experience, involves depths of meanings yet to be penetrated. Transcending apprehensions bring an awareness of further possibilities and moments of transcendence bring momentary richness of life into the victim's experience. When subjective understandings, preserved through forgetfulness, repression, or distortion, are challenged by further encounters, reality confronts with an insistence that creates conflict and demands full justice to that which is encountered. The destruction of self-understanding that has occurred through abuse goes beyond exposing personal and social vulnerabilities, and touches existential ambiguities at the core of the person's being, which cries out for ground, meaning, purpose, security, completeness, certainty, and peace.

Healing Occurs Relationally

Created in the image of God, human beings are ontologically relational in nature, and, as such, the human soul longs for relationship where acceptance, belonging, and love are experienced. The fundamental need of every child is to be in the loving community of family for healthy human development to occur. The fundamental need of every Christian believer is participation in church life and community for healthy spiritual development to occur. The community is crucial in the process of identity formation.

The human spirit, as transformational, points outward in search of loving relationships. As such, the psycho-spiritual needs arising in the victim will not be silenced until they begin to be dialogically addressed. The growth tendency in the human spirit toward expansion and wholeness is best facilitated in an environment of love where empathetic dialogue facilitates the creative capacity of the spirit to bring change and development in the person. The directional tendency of the spirit toward fellowship and loving relationship is ultimately a search for the perfect community of love.

Experiencing God's saving love leads to a new sociality, a community of people sharing a common salvation and mediating a new transcending story, within which epistemic transformation in relation to identity and destiny take place. A new belonging means a new becoming.

Human Help is Limited

When any relationship, inside or outside the church, personal or professional, is characterized by genuineness, empathy, and unconditional positive regard, the core conditions exist for a deeper trust and connection; whereby, it is safe for the genuine person to emerge and, in the exchange, find some therapeutic benefit.

In these moments, the victim experiences some contact with reality, giving rise to a level of clarity which allows reconnecting, reinterpreting, and resolving to occur and result in some measure of relief.

This process, while helpful to a degree, is unable to attain resolution for the existential issues and conflicts raised by the victim's experiences. At best, these relationships can point to and foster the desire for, or the conviction of, a perfect and fully trustworthy love in which openness becomes surrender and means safety.

Divine Love Opens New Possibilities

While loving human persons can be attentive, understanding, non-judgmental, and supportive toward the disclosing victim, no human person can reach the place of deepest intimacy with another. Their love is really neither unconditional, their understanding complete, nor their availability total. Human help has limitations. In the divine, however, intimacy has no limit or barrier.

The infinite God is unlimited in love and availability and with full and complete insight always. This means there is the possibility that an abiding acceptance, valuing, and help can be experienced.

Within the Christian victim finds the one who sees more, in regard to their true-self and their many selves, than they. This one can disclose the-self and selves fully, even to their surprise and acknowledgment, while loving them completely and constantly.

The health-inducing potential of this revelation can be likened to sight for the blind, hearing for the deaf, prison doors being opened, and chains being broken so captives can be set free. God expels the darkness of pain, hopelessness, and helplessness through an intimate knowing and love.

God is Relational Through the Spirit

The Spirit is the bond of unity between Father and the Son, between God and believers in Christ, and between Christians in the community of the church.

In proceeding from the Father to the Son and then returning to the Father, the Spirit both "reveals to them their respective identities" and "constitutes their community."[3] The Spirit reveals to the Father and Son their difference and unity. The Spirit reveals the Father as Father to the Son and the Son as Son to the Father and, in so doing, discloses, displays, and realizes their intimate community with each other.

The incarnate Christ was further empowered by the Spirit to be the revelation of this bond of unity between the Father and the Son. It is the Spirit who reveals that intimate relationship to human beings and brings them into participation with the divine community of love. As such, the Spirit reveals this divine communion, its presence in the world, and the opening up of divine relations for human participation and the unity of human and divine relations.

The Spirit Facilitates Healing

The relational wholeness of Jesus Christ means the human and Holy Spirit are made for each other, and that the Holy Spirit is the means whereby this same relational wholeness can be reproduced in human beings. This

---

3. Oberdorfer, "The Holy Spirit," 36.

Spirit-to-spirit embrace is a connection in the depth of one's innermost being bringing an intimate unity with transformational potential. Divine love enables the transformation of the human self as a child of God, meaning a new identity, security, and potential for growth and well-being.

The opening up, realization, and abiding nature of this life-giving union is the work of the Spirit. The Spirit is the quickening, activating, and actualizing personal power of new life. The Spirit redefines life in the present and the future. There is both a new beginning and a progressive growth and progress toward the realization of spiritual maturity as seen in Christ, the perfect human.

Spiritual union and growth then mean the healing or re-humanizing of the human person. The Christian's being is in becoming Christ-like in and through the Spirit. Movement in and through the Spirit toward that end means the undoing and overcoming of bondages, blockages, and barriers into greater freedom, well-being, and growth. The potential, hope, and actualizing of spiritual healing for personal growth is in and through the Spirit.

Cooperation with the Spirit Enables Healing

While spiritual healing and growth are in and through the Spirit, the victim does contribute to their own ongoing transformation. Once the Spirit has awakened new energies for liberation and growth within the recovering believer, a human response is still required for healing and growth to be progressively realized. Transformation is empowered by human choices made in accordance with the will of the Spirit.

While it is the Spirit who initiates the possibility and potential for liberation, change, and growth (and persuades, encourages, and challenges for the making of choices resonant with the will of the Spirit), the victim must yield to this newly created alternative orientation. In yielding to the will of the Spirit, the victim is affirming the all-good and all-wise purpose of God for their life and progress and so enabling the Spirit to move in and for them.

This spiritual and healing journey involves a leaving of old securities and modes of being, as well as a cleaving to the goodwill and purpose of the all-sufficient power and strength of God, to effect radical change that liberates, enriches, fulfills, and completes. For the victim, cooperation with the Spirit is the only way into a personally experienced freedom and health-of-being.

Inner Healing is Outwardly Observable

In his letter to the Galatians, Paul maintains that the Spirit working in the believer's life will produce the positive attributes of a godly character, which were evident in Jesus as recorded in the gospels. He says the fruit of the Spirit is love, joy, peace, patience, kindness, goodness, faithfulness, gentleness, and self-control (Gal 5:22).

The victim's life prior to experiencing healing was variously characterized by a sense of isolation, loss, shame, guilt, grief, hatred, lack of trust, and despair. It is only the Holy Spirit who can resolve the spiritual-existential conflicts underlying this condition by making the knowledge of God and the reality intended by God accessible to the victim.

When the victim is touched by the spiritual presence of Christ, they know themselves to be loved and valuable, and love comes to life in them. As inner healing and renewal take place, the deep emotions of gratitude, confidence, compassion, and hope grow and find expression within the context of a relationship with God, the church, and the world. These become abiding dispositions which characterize the recovered victim and dispose them toward God and others in a way that is approximating their source in the Spirit and their goal in Christ.

Confidence in the Spirit Empowers Ministry

The recovered victim knows themselves to have been healed through the work of the Holy Spirit. The recovered victim is furthermore convinced that their condition was beyond human help, that theirs was a spiritual problem in need of spiritual help. Hence their choices were limited to either remaining in their woundedness or depending upon the person and work of the Spirit to bring about their healing.

This recognition of human limitations necessitated openness to the will and power of the Spirit which proved to be efficacious. This total dependence upon the Holy Spirit as the source and power of their progress cultivated a confidence in and reliance upon the Spirit in all aspects of Christian ministry.

Christian Ministry is the Work of the Spirit

There is much in church work that can be done in and through human capacity, where God is asked to support and sustain that which is self-initiated and implemented. However, genuine Christian ministry occurs when human beings are attentive, obedient, and reliant upon the will and work of the Holy Spirit.

The personal presence and operation of the Holy Spirit in a believer's life is indispensable to their growth and development as persons-in-Christ. It is essential for victims of childhood sexual abuse that counselors and prayer ministers involved in the recovery process have personal experience with depending and confiding in the Holy Spirit for healing, if it is to be facilitated and actualized.

Theology and experience teach that the Holy Spirit is the redemptive activity available through Christian ministry as part of his Trinitarian purpose. God's future is being realized through and by the Spirit personally and historically. In terms of recovery, the participants describe the Holy Spirit in terms of "the safe place," "the comforter" who is "revealing" and "guiding."

The disposition of the Christian minister toward the Holy Spirit then should be one of dependence, expectancy, attentiveness, sensitivity, and co-operation, and toward the victims as attentive, loving, caring, unimposing, and full of hope.

Implications for Pastoral Education

Based on this research, a number of implications are important in the training of pastors and pastoral carers.

1. Pastoral educators should include the voices of recovered victims in relation to pastoral theology. They are pioneers in facing the depth of the human condition. Their healing process has led them to a chasm of chaos. Their perspectives may well challenge traditional theologies and practice. They are well able to highlight the unhelpful, hurtful, and harmful effects of simplistic theology.

    They have had to reconcile their suffering and pain with the idea of a good and all-powerful God who didn't intervene in their plight. They have had to come to grips with the complex nature of forgiveness. They have had to discover the meaning and benefits of intimacy with God. They have had to recover the meaning and value of trust, love, and hope.

2. Pastors and pastoral carers need to be ready for the psychological and existential needs of victims. The pastor can be the first person a victim turns to for support. Pastors should be willing to, and see the benefit in, collaborating with other professionals and they should know whom to contact for help outside ministry.

3. Pastors and pastoral carers need to be aware that victims may experience post-traumatic stress symptoms, lack of trust, and religious trauma. Pastors need to increase their knowledge of the problem and be aware of the devastation of childhood sexual abuse to the victim. One must assume that there are victims in every congregation. Among the victims there may be those who have experienced recovery, are in recovery, are still suffering, have never disclosed their abuse, or may not yet remember the abuse.

4. Pastors need to reflect upon the problem both theologically and psychologically. Pastors should engage in further studies in psychology and the psychology of religion.

5. Pastors and pastoral carers need to be able to fully integrate the person and work of the Holy Spirit into their theory and practice. The pneumatic component must be at the heart of pastoral care and counseling.

6. Local churches need to be safe places for victims to find healing. As healing for victims is a spiritual and relational process, pastors and carers need to explore ways in which people are able to connect in order to facilitate healing.

Concluding Statement

In this book, I have said nothing new beyond what every recovered victim of childhood sexual abuse who is a Christian already knows by experience and personal history. But what I did want to do is to explore at a deeper level the human experience of the Holy Spirit's work in bringing restoration and healing.

And with this deepening, this opening up of the phenomenon of the work of the Spirit concealed within the underlying structures of healing, comes the necessity to make it known through a process of uncovering or naming the underlying themes of meaning. The healing journeys listened to and explicated herein disclose the elements of the Spirit's work underlying the healing process. Hopefully, this will help better inform ministerial practice.

APPENDIX 1

Interview Questions

THE LIST OF QUESTIONS prepared for the interview was as follows:
Age range
Gender
Marital status
Denomination

1. Can you tell me about your spiritual journey?
2. I understand that you have been sexually abused.
    a. Over what time period did the abuse extend?
    b. How did your life change because of what happened?
    c. What impact did this have on you?
    d. How did you try to deal with the problems you experienced?
3. When did you begin to talk with someone about the abuse?
4. How did you feel when you told your story?
5. What did healing involve for you?
6. Where was God in all of this?
7. Would you please share your journey toward healing?
8. Are there any special or significant times in your journey toward healing?
9. How would you describe the spiritual element of your journey toward healing?

Appendix 1

10. In what way was the Holy Spirit involved in your journey towards healing?
11. Where do you think you are in your journey toward healing?
12. What advice would you give to someone seeking healing from childhood sexual abuse?

When appropriate, I asked additional questions such as: "Are you able to talk some more about that?"; "Is there anything else you feel is important?"; "Can you share your feelings in relation to that?"; and "How do you understand that?" in order to allow deeper access to the participants' experiences.

APPENDIX 2

Two articles by Holroyd[1] and Devenish[2] (April 2002, online) provided a phenomenological methodological approach to explicating human experience based on Schweitzer's (1998) adaption of Giorgi (1997) involving six stages as follows:

Stage 1: Achieve an intuitive/holistic understanding of the data from the interviews by attending to the transcripts while bracketing our preconceptions and judgments.

Stage 2: Form a constituent profile of each participant from the raw data and summarize in a three-stepped process. Natural meaning units (NMUs) are identified.[3] The NMUs are reduced to central themes (CTs). The CTs are reconstituted to form a constituent profile.

Stage 3: Form a thematic index by delineating constituent profiles, extracting specific words that highlight the meaning of the experience (referents), and establishing a thematic file index.

Stage 4: Search the thematic index comparing referents, central themes, and constituent profiles to form interpretative themes.

Stage 5: Arrive at extended descriptions by providing a rigorous description of the interpretative themes from the data.

Stage 6: Synthesize the extended descriptions by summarizing the interpretative themes to produce a succinct in-depth description of the participant's experience in relation to the relevant phenomena.

---

1. Holroyd, "Phenomenological Research."
2. Devenish, "An Applied Method."
3. NMUs are expressions that have a single meaning.

APPENDIX 3

The Research Key

1. Spiritual Journey
    1.1. upbringing/family history/background
    1.2. early memories/experiences
    1.3. significant (early) events recalled
    1.4. contact with Church, God, Bible
    1.5. search for meaning/truth
    1.6. spiritual experiences/insights/encounters/impressions/struggles
    1.7. sense of calling/purpose/hope
    1.8. view of God, Jesus, the Holy Spirit
    1.9. view of self/world/Bible/Church
    1.10. important people/influences/events/experiences/resources
    1.11. church involvement/memories/experiences/times
    1.12. marriage and family
2. Abuse
    2.1. memories of abuse
        2.1.1 nature/severity/length/extent/frequency/emotional effects of the abuse
        2.1.2. perpetrators/relationship with/number
        2.1.3. related events
    2.2. initial impressions/understanding of abuse experiences
    2.3. view of God the Father, Jesus, Holy Spirit
    2.4. view of self/others/world

Appendix 3

    2.4.1. view of Bible/Church
  2.5. impact of the abuse/problems/associations/consequences
  2.6. coping methods
  2.7. awareness, understanding, naming and disclosure
    2.7.1. effect of
    2.7.2. related issues/events
3. Recovery/Healing
  3.1. attempts at recovery/choices
  3.2. significant times/resources/moments of healing
  3.3. significant people
  3.4. changes identified
  3.5. spiritual dimension
    3.5.1. involvement of God, Jesus, Holy Spirit
    3.5.2. involvement with Church/Bible/Christians/others
    3.5.3. spiritual issues/observations
  3.6. views of God/Jesus/Holy Spirit
    3.6.1. related issues
  3.7. view of world/self/church/others
  3.8. important elements in healing
    3.8.1. process/event

BIBLIOGRAPHY

Allen, E. A. "What Is the Church's Healing Ministry?" *International Review of Mission* 90 (2001) 46.
Allender, Dan. *The Wounded Heart: Hope for Adult Victims of Childhood Sexual Abuse*. Colorado Springs: Navpress, 1990.
Anderson, Ray S. *Ministry on the Fireline: A Practical Theology for an Empowered Church*. Downers Grove, IL: InterVarsity, 1993.
Ashbrook, James B. *Minding the Soul: Pastoral Counseling as Remembering*. Minneapolis: Fortress, 1996.
Atwood, George E., and Robert D. Stolorow. *Structures of Subjectivity: Explorations in Psychoanalytic Phenomenology*. Hillsdale, NJ: Analytic, 1984.
Au, Wilkie, and Noreen Cannon. *Urgings of the Heart: A Spirituality of Integration*. New York: Paulist, 1995.
Aulén, Gustaf. *Chritus Victor: An Historical Study of the Three Main Types of the Idea of the Atonement*. London: SPCK, 1931.
Bachelard, Sarah. "Foolishness to the Greeks: Plantinga and the Epistemology of Christian Belief." *Sophia* 48 (2009) 105–18.
Baker, Mark D., and Joel B. Green. *Recovering the Scandal of the Cross: Atonement in the New Testament and Contemporary Contexts*. Downers Grove, IL: InterVarsity, 2011.
Barker, Patrick M. "The Relevance of James Loder's Grammar of Transformation for Pastoral Care and Counseling." *Journal of Pastoral Care* 49 (1995) 158–66.
Barth, Karl. *The Epistle to the Romans*. London: Oxford University Press, 1933.
Beck, Aaron T. *Cognitive Therapy of Depression*. New York: Guildord, 1979.
Beck, T. D. "The Divine Dis-Comforter: The Holy Spirit's Role in Transformative." *Journal of Spiritual Formation & Soul Care* 2 (2009) 199–218.
Beker, J. Christiaan. *Paul the Apostle: The Triumph of God in Life and Thought*. Minneapolis: Fortress, 1980.
Belzen, Jacob A., and Antoon Geels. *Autobiography and the Psychological Study of Religious Lives*. Amsterdam: Rodopi, 2008.
Benner, David G. *Psychotherapy and the Spiritual Tradition*. Grand Rapids: Baker, 1988.
———. *Sacred Companions: The Gift of Spiritual Friendship & Direction*. Downers Grove, IL: InterVarsity, 2002.
———. *Care of Souls: Revisioning Christian Nurture and Counsel*. Ada, MI: Baker, 2004.
———. *Surrender to Love: Discovering the Heart of Christian Spirituality*: Downers Grove, IL: InterVarsity, 2015.
Bion, Wilfred R. *Elements of Psychoanalysis*. London: Heinemann, 1963.

Bibliography

Bloesch, Donald G. *The Holy Spirit: Works and Gifts.* Downers Grove, IL: InterVarsity, 2000.

Boisen, Anton T. *The Exploration of the Inner World.* Chicago and New York: Willett, Clark & Co., 1936.

Bolsinger, Tod E. "It Takes a Church to Raise a Christian: How the Community of God Transforms Lives." *Missiology* 33 (2005) 117–19.

Boyd, Jeffrey H. *Reclaiming the Soul: The Search for Meaning in a Self-Centered Culture.* Cleveland, OH: Pilgrim, 1996.

Briere, John, and Marsha Runtz. "Suicidal Thoughts and Behaviours in Former Sexual Abuse Victims." *Canadian Journal of Behavioural Science* 4 (1986) 413–23.

Broadbent, A., and R. Bentley. *Child Abuse and Neglect Australia 1995–96.* Australian Institute of Health and Welfare, Canberra, 1997.

Browne, A., and D. Finkelhor. "Impact of Child Sexual Abuse: A Review of the Research." *Psychological Bulletin* 99 (1986) 66.

Brueggemann, Walter B. *Praying the Psalms: Engaging Scripture and the Life of the Spirit.* Eugene, OR: Wipf & Stock, 2007.

Brunner, Emil. *The Misunderstanding of the Church.* Cambridge: Lutterworth, 1952.

Bultmann, Rudolph. *Theology of the New Testament.* Translated by Kendrick Grobel. London: SCM, 1965.

———. "The New Testament and Theology." In *Kerygma and Myth*, vol.1, edited by H. W. Bartch, 1–44. New York: Harper & Row, 1953.

Chia, Roland. "Trinity and Ontology: Colin Gunton's Ecclesiology." *International Journal of Systematic Theology* 9 (2007) 452–68.

Clifford, Richard, and Khaled Anatolios. "Christian Salvation: Biblical and Theological Perspectives." *Theological Studies* 66 (2005) 739–69.

Clough, William R. "To Be Loved and to Love." *Journal of Psychology & Theology* 34 (2006) 23–31.

Conn, Walter E. "Self-Transcendence, the True Self, and Self Love." *Pastoral Pschology* 46 (1998) 323–31.

Conradie, E. M. "Healing in Soteriological Perspective." *Religion & Theology* 13 (2006) 3–22.

Conte, J. R., and J. R. Schuerman. "Factors Associated with an Increased Impact of Child Sexual Abuse." *Child Abuse & Neglect* 11 (1987) 201–11.

Courtois, C. A. "Healing the Incest Wound: A Treatment Update with Attention to Recovered-Memory Issues." *American Journal of Psychotherapy* 51 (1997) 464.

———. "The Sexual After-Effects of Incest/Child Sexual Abuse." *SIECUS Report* 29 (2000) 11.

Crabb, Lawrence. *Connecting: A Radical New Vision.* Nashville, TN: Word Publishing, 1997.

Cross, T. L. "The Divine-Human Encounter towards a Pentecostal Theology of Experience." *Pneuma* 31 (2009) 3–34.

Crowley, M. Sue, *The Search for Autonomous Intimacy: Sexual Abuse and Young Women's Identity Development.* New York: Peter Lang, 2000.

Devenish, Stuart. "An Applied Method for Undertaking Phenomenological Explication of Interview Transcripts." *Indo-Pacific Journal of Phenomenology* 2 (2002) 1–20.

Dodds, Adam. "The Mission of the Spirit and the Mission of the Church: Towards a Trinitarian Missiology." *Evangelical Review of Theology* 35 (2011) 209–26.

Bibliography

Doehring, Carrie. *Internal Desecration: Traumatization and Representations of God.* Lanham, MD: University Press of America, 1993.

———. *Taking Care: Monitoring Power Dynamics and Relational Boundaries in Pastoral Care and Counseling.* Nashville: Abingdon, 1995.

———. *The Practice of Pastoral Care: A Postmodern Approach.* Louisville: Westminster John Knox, 2006.

Dresser, Horatio W. *The Philosophy of the Spirit: A Study of the Spiritual Nature of Man and the Presence of God, with a Supplementary Essay on the Logic of Hegel.* New York: G. P. Putnam's Sons, 1908.

Driver, John. *Understanding the Atonement for the Mission of the Church.* Scottdale, PA: Herald, 1986.

Dunn, James D. G. *Unity and Diversity in the New Testament: An Inquiry into the Character of Earliest Christianity.* London: SCM, 2006.

Edwards, Denis. *Human Experience of God.* New York: Paulist, 1983.

Engelbrecht, Ben. "The Indwelling of the Holy Spirit, Pt 1 : An Evaluation of Contemporary Pneumatologby." *Journal of Theology for Southern Africa* 30 (March 1980) 19–33.

Erikson, Erik H., and Joan M. Erikson. *The Life Cycle Completed.* New York: Norton, 1982.

Falsetti, S. A. et al. "Treatment of Posttraumatic Stress Disorder with Comorbid Panic Attacks: Combining Cognitive Processing Therapy with Panic Control Treatment Techniques." *Group Dynamics: Theory, Research, and Practice* 5 (2001) 252–60.

Fichter, Joseph Henry. *Healing Ministries: Conversations on the Spiritual Dimensions of Health Care.* New York: Paulist, 1986.

Fiddes, Paul S. *Participating in God: A Pastoral Doctrine of the Trinity.* Louisville: Westminster John Knox, 2000.

Finkelhor, David. *Child Sexual Abuse: New Theory and Research.* New York: Free, 1984.

Finlan, Stephen. *Problems with Atonement: The Origins of, and Controversy about, the Atonement Doctrine.* Collegeville, MN: Liturgical, 2005.

Fowler, James W. *Faith Development and Pastoral Care.* London: Fortress, 1987.

Fromm, Erich. *The Art of Loving.* London: HarperCollins, 1957.

Gall, Terry Lynn et al., "Spirituality and the Current Adjustment of Adult Survivors of Childhood Sexual Abuse." *Journal for the Scientific Study of Religion* 46 (2007) 101–17.

Ganje-Fling, Marilyn A., and Patricia McCarthy. "Impact of Childhood Sexual Abuse on Client Spiritual Development: Counseling Implications." *Journal of Counseling & Development* 74 (1996) 253.

Gerkin, Charles V. *The Living Human Document: Re-Visioning Pastoral Counseling in a Hermeneutical Mode.* Nashville: Abingdon, 1984.

Ghent, Emmanuel. "Masochism, Submission, Surrender: Masochism as a Perversion of Surrender." *Contemporary Psychoanalysis* 26 (1990) 108–35.

Giorgi, A. "The Theory, Practice, and Evaluation of the Phenomenological Method as a Qualitative Research Method." *Journal of Phenomenological Psychology* 28 (1997) 236–60.

———. "Difficulties Encountered in the Application of the Phenomenological Method in the Social Sciences." *The Indo-Pacific Journal of Phenomenology* 8 (2008) 1–9.

———. "The Descriptive Phenomenological Psychological Method." *Journal of Phenomenological Psychology* 43 (2012) 3–12.

Girard, Rene. *The Scapegoat.* Baltimore: John Hopkins University Press, 1986.

Bibliography

Goldblatt, P. "Stories of Longing and Rememberance: The Role of Myth in Making Meaning." *Multicultural Review* 19 (2010) 37–41.

Gould, J. B. "Spiritual Healing of Disrupted Childhood." *The Journal of Pastoral Care and Counseling* 60 (2006) 263–73.

Granberg-Michaelson, Karin. "Reclaiming the Healing Ministry of the Church." *International Review of Mission* 90 (2001) 134.

Grant, Robert. *The Way of the Wound: A Spirituality of Trauma and Transformation*. N.p.: n.p., n.d.

Green, Joel B. *Salvation*. St. Louis: Chalice, 2003.

———. "Kaleidoscopic View." In *The Nature of the Atonement: Four Views* edited by James Beilby and Paul R. Eddy, 157–96. Downers Grove, IL: InterVarsity, 2006.

Grenz, Stanley J. *Theology for the Community of God*. Carlisle, England: Paternoster, 1994.

———. *Created for Community: Connecting Christian Belief with Christian Living*. Grand Rapids: Baker, 2004.

Gunton, Colin E. *On Being the Church: Essays on the Christian Community*. Edinburgh: T. & T. Clark, 1989.

———. *Act and Being: Towards a Theology of Divine Attributes*. London: SCM, 2002.

———. *The Promise of Trinitarian Theology*. New York: T. & T. Clark, 2006.

Haight, R. "Jesus and Salvation: An Essay in Interpretation." *Theological Studies* 55 (1994) 225–52.

Hart, Patrick, and Jonathan Montaldo. *The Intimate Merton: His Life from His Journals*. San Francisco: HarperCollins, 1999.

Heidegger, Martin. *Pathmarks*. Cambridge: Cambridge University Press, 1998.

———. *Being and Time*. New York: Harper & Row, 1962.

Hendry, G. S. *The Holy Spirit in Christian Theology*. Philadelphia: Westminster, 1956.

Herman, Judith L. *Trauma and Recovery*. New York: Basic Books, 1992.

Herman et al., "Long-term Effects of Incestuous Abuse in Childhood." *The American Journal of Psychiatry* 143 (1986) 1293–96.

Hiltner, Seward. *Self-Understanding Through Psychology and Religion*. New York: Scribner's, 1951.

———. *Preface to Pastoral Theology*. Nashville: Abingdon, 1958.

———. *Theological Dynamics*. Nashville: Abingdon, 1972.

Holroyd, C. "Phenomenological Research Method, Design and Procedure: A Phenomenological Investigation of Being-in-Community as Experienced by Two Individuals Who Have Participated in a Community Building Workshop." *Indo-Pacific Journal of Phenomenology* 1 (2001) 1–10.

Hultgren, A. J. "Salvation: Its Forms and Dynamics in the New Testament." *Dialog: A Journal of Theology* 45 (2006) 215–22.

Humphrey, Edith McEwan. *Ecstasy and Intimacy: When the Holy Spirit Meets the Human Spirit*. Grand Rapids: Eerdmans, 2006.

Hunsinger, G. "The Daybreak of the New Creation: Christ's Resurrection in Recent Theology." *Scottish Journal of Theology* 57 (2004) 163–81.

Husserl, Edmund. *The Crisis of European Sciences and Transcendental Phenomenology: An Introduction to Phenomenological Philosophy*. Evanston, IL: Northwestern University Press, 1970.

Imbens, Annie, and Ineke Jonker. *Christianity and Incest*. Minneapolis: Fortress, 1992.

Inhelder, Barbel, and Jean Piaget. *The Early Growth of Logic in the Child: Classification and Seriation*. New York: Harper & Row, 1964.

Bibliography

Jackson, A. P., and S. J. Sears. "Implications of an Africentric Worldview in Reducing Stress for African American Women." *Journal of Counseling & Development* 71 (1992) 184–90.

Josselson, Ruthellen. *Finding Herself: Pathways to Identity Development in Women.* San Francisco: Jossey-Bass, 1987.

———. *Revising Herself: The Story of Women's Identity from College to Midlife.* New York: Oxford University Press, 1996.

Kainen, Veli-Matti. *Toward a Pneumatological Theology: Pentecostal and Ecumenical Perspectives on Ecclesiology, Soteriology, and Theology of Mission.* Lanham, MD: University Press of America, 2002.

———. "Spirit, Reconciliation and Healing in the Community: Missiological Insights from Pentecostals." *International Review of Mission* 94 (2005) 43–50.

Kelleman, Robert W. *Soul Physicians: A Theology of Soul Care and Spiritual Direction.* Winona Lake, IN: BMH Books, 2007.

Kelsey, Morton T. *Encounter with God: A Theology of Christian Experience.* Minneapolis: Bethany Fellowship, 1972.

Kendall-Tackett, K., L. M. Williams, and D. Finkelhor. "Impact of Sexual Abuse on Children: A Review and Synthesis of Recent Empirical Studies." *Psychological Bulletin* 113 (1993) 164.

Kennedy, J. E., R. C. Davis, and B. G. Taylor. "Changes in Spirituality and Well-Being among Victims of Sexual Assault." *Journal for the Scientific Study of Religion* 37 (1998) 322–28.

Kierkegaard, Soren. *The Sickness unto Death.* Princeton: Princeton University Press, 1941.

Kinsey, A. et al. *Sexual Behavior in the Human Female.* Philadelphia: W.B. Saunders, 1953.

Klein, Melanie. "The Origins of Transference." In *The Writings of Melanie Klein*, 57–63. London: Hogarth, 1975.

Knight, Douglas H. *The Eschatological Economy: Time and the Hospitality of God.* Grand Rapids: Eerdmans, 2006.

Koenig, H. G., M. E. McCullough, and D. B. Larson. *Handbook of Religion and Health.* New York: Oxford University Press, 2001.

Kydd, R. A. N. *Healing Through the Centuries: Models for Understanding.* Peabody, MA: Hendrickson, 1998.

LaCugna, Catherine Mowry. *God for Us: The Trinity and Christian Life.* New York: HarperCollins, 1991.

Ladd, George Eldon. *The Presence of the Future: The Eschatology of Biblical Realism.* Grand Rapids: Eerdmans, 1980.

Lamborn, A. B. "Who Will Stir the Water for Us? A Pastoral Retrospective." *Pastoral Psychology* 56 (2007) 165–76.

Lamont, A. "Effects of Child Abuse and Neglect for Adult Survivors." Australian Institute of Family Studies, 2010.

Langberg, Diane M. *On the Threshold of Hope: Opening the Door to Healing for Survivors of Sexual Abuse.* Wheaton, IL: Tyndale House, 1999.

Lemke, J. "Across the Scales of Time: Artificats, Activities and Meanings in Ecosocial Systems." *Mind, Culture and Activity* 7 (2000) 273–90.

Lemoncelli, J., and A. Carey. "The Psychospiritual Dynamics of Adult Survivors of Abuse." *Counseling & Values* 40 (1996) 175–84.

Levinas, E. "Useless Suffering." In *The Problem of Evil*, edited by Mark Larrimore, 371–74. Oxford: Blackwell, 2001.

BIBLIOGRAPHY

Loder, James E. *The Transforming Moment*. 2nd vol. Colorado Springs: Helmers & Howard., 1989.

———. *The Logic of the Spirit: Human Development in Theological Perspective*. New York: John Wiley & Sons, 1998.

———. "The Great Sex Charade and the Loss of Intimacy." *Word & World* 21 (2001) 81–87.

Loder, J. E., and J. W. Fowler. "Conversations on Fowler's Stages of Faith and Loder's The Transforming Moment." *Religious Education* 77 (1982) 133–48.

Long, E. T. "Suffering and Transcendence." *International Journal of Philosophy and Religion* 60 (2006) 139–48.

Lull, D. J. "The Spirit and the Creative Transformation of Human Existence." *Journal of the American Academy of Religion* 47 (1979) 39–55.

Macchia, F. D. "The Spirit of Life and the Spirit of Immortality: An Appreciative Review of Levison's Filled with the Spirit." *Pneuma: The Journal of the Society for Pentecostal Studies* 33 (2011) 69–78.

MacNutt, Francis. *Healing Through Prayer*. New York: Bantam, 1977.

———. *Overcome by the Spirit*. New York: Fleming H. Revell, 1990.

Marshall, Molly T. *Joining the Dance: A Theology for the Spirit*. Valley Forge, PA: Judson, 2003.

Maslow, A. *Motivation and Personality*. New York: Harper & Row, 1970.

Matera, Frank J. "Christ in the Theologies of Paul and John: A Study in the Diverse Unity of New Testament Theology." *Theological Studies* 67 (2006) 237–56.

May, Rollo. *The Cry for Myth*. New York: W. W. Norton, 1991.

McNeill, John T. *A History of the Cure of Souls*. New York: Harper & Row, 1977.

Means, J. Jeffrey *Trauma & Evil: Healing the Wounded Soul*. Minneapolis: Fortress, 2000.

Meek, E. L. *Loving to Know: Introducing Covenant Epistemology*. Eugene, OR: Cascade, 2011.

Meiselman, K. C. *Incest: A Psychological Study of Causes and Effects with Treatment Recommendations*. San Francisco: Jossey-Bass, 1978.

Merton, Thomas. *The Inner Experience: Notes on Contemplation*. New York: HarperCollins, 2003.

Miner, M. H. "Back to the Basics in Attachment to God: Revisiting Theory in Light of Theology." *Journal of Psychology & Theology* 35 (2007) 112–22.

Moltmann, Jurgen. *The Way of Jesus Christ: Christology in Messianic Dimensions*. London: SCM, 1990.

———. *The Spirit of Life: A Universal Affirmation*. London: SCM, 1992.

———. *The Source of Life: The Holy Spirit and the Theology of Life*. Minneapolis: Fortress, 1997.

———. *The Church in the Power of the Spirit*. Munich: SCM, 1998.

———. "The Blessing of Hope: The Theology of Hope and the Full Gospel of Life." *Journal of Pentecostal Theology* 13 (2005) 147–61.

———. *Experiences of God*. Minneapolis: Fortress, 2007.

———. "The Presence of God's Future: The Risen Christ." *Anglican Theological Review* 89 (2007) 577–88.

Moon, G. W. "How God Is Good for the Soul." *Journal of Psychology & Christianity* 22 (2003) 78–88.

Moon, G. W., and D. G. Benner. *Spiritual Direction and the Care of Souls*. Downers Grove, IL: InterVarsity, 2004.

Bibliography

Moore, M. "Teaching Justice and Reconciliation in a Wounding World." In *The Other Side of Sin: Woundedness from the Perspective of the Sinned-Against*, edited by S. A. Park and S. L. Nelson, 143–63. New York: State University of New York Press, 2001.

Mostert, C. "The Kingdom Anticipated: The Church and Eschatology." *International Journal of Systematic Theology* 13 (2011) 25–37.

Mullen, P. E., and J. Fleming. "Long-Term Effects of Child Sexual Abuse." https://aifs.gov.au/cfca/publications/long-term-effects-child-sexual-abuse-1998.

Nel, Marius. "The Way to Healing: Faith and Prayer." *Spirit and Church* 2 (2000) 247–64.

Nelson, Susan L. "Facing Evil: Evil's Many Faces." *Interpretation* 57 (2003) 398–413.

———. "For Shame, For Shame, The Shame of it All: Postures of Refusal and the Broken Heart." In *The Other Side of Sin: Woundedness from the Perspective of the Sinned-Against*, edited by A. S. Park and S. L. Nelson, 71–86. New York: State University of New York Press, 2001.

Newbigin, Lesslie. *Trinitarian Doctrine for Today's Mission*. Carlisle, England: Paternoster, 1998.

Nouwen, H. J. *Lifesigns: Intimacy, Fecundity, and Ecstasy in Christian Perspective*. New York: Doubleday, 1986.

———. *The Wounded Healer: Ministry in Contemporary Society*. London: Darton Longman & Todd, 2000.

Oates, W. E. "Holy Spirit as Counsellor." *Review & Expositor* 54 (1957) 233–45.

———. *The Presence of God in Pastoral Counseling*. Texas: Word Publishing, 1986.

Oberdorfer, B. "The Holy Spirit - a Person? Reflection on the Spirit's Trinitarian Identity." In *The Work of the Spirit: Pneumatology and Pentecostalism*, edited by Michael Welker, 27–46. Grand Rapids: Eerdmans, 2006.

Oden, T. C. *Pastoral Theology: Essentials of Ministry*. New York: HarperCollins, 1983.

———. *Care of Souls in the Classic Tradition*. Minneapolis: Fortress, 1984.

O'Donohue, John. *Anam Cara: Spiritual Wisdom from the Celtic World*. London: Bantam, 1997.

———. *Eternal Echoes: Exploring Our Hunger to Belong*. London: Bantam, 2000.

Pacot, Simone. *Evangélisation des Profondeurs*. Paris: Points, 1997.

Pannenburg, Wolfhart. *Jesus—God and Man*. Philadelphia: Westminister, 1974.

Pargament, K. I., Gina M. Magyar-Russell, and Nichole A. Murray-Swank. "The Sacred and the Search for Significance: Religion as a Unique Process." *Journal of Social Issues* 61 (2005) 665–87.

Pargament, K. I., and S. M. Saunders. "Introduction to the Special Issue on Spirituality and Psychotherapy." *Journal of Clinical Psychology* 63 (2007) 903–07.

Park, A. S. "The Bible and Han." In *The Other Side of Sin: Woundedness from the Perspective of the Sinned-Against*, edited by A. S. Park and S. L. Nelson, 45–59. New York: State University of New York Press, 2001.

Parker, S. "Winnicott's Object Relations Theory and the Work of the Holy Spirit." *Journal of Psychology & Theology* 36 (2008) 285–93.

Paolucci et al. "A Meta-Analysis of the Published Research on the Effects of Child Sexual Abuse." *Journal of Psychology* 135 (2001) 17–36.

Parlow, S. B. "Personal Transformation in Karl Rahner's Christianity: Constructed by Love." *Psychoanalytic Inquiry* 28 (2008) 570–79.

Patton, John. *Pastoral Care in Context: An Introduction to Pastoral Care*. Louisville: Westminster John Knox, 1993.

Peck, M. Scott. *The Road Less Travelled*. London: Arrow Books, 1990.

Bibliography

Pembroke, Neil. *Moving Toward Spiritual Maturity: Psychological, Contemplative and Moral Challenges in Christian Living.* New York: Haworth Pastoral Press, 2007.

Peters, T. "Six Ways of Salvation: How Does Jesus Save?" *Dialog: A Journal of Theology* 45 (2006) 223–35.

Phillips, A., and J. C. Daniluk. "Beyond 'Survivor': How Childhood Sexual Abuse Informs the Identity of Adult Women at the End of the Therapeutic Process." *Journal of Counseling and Development: JCD* 82 (2004) 177–84.

Pinnock, Clark H. *Flame of Love: A Theology of the Holy Spirit.* Downers Grove, IL: InterVarsity, 1996.

Polyani, Michael. *Personal Knowledge: Toward a Post-Critical Philosophy.* London: Routledge & K. Paul, 1958.

Porterfield, Amanda. *Healing in the History of Christianity.* New York: Oxford University Press, 2005.

Potter, P. "Healing and Salvation." *Ecumenical Review* 33 (1981) 330–40.

Price-Robertson et al., "The Prevalence of Child Abuse and Neglect." https://aifs.gov.au/cfca/publications/prevalence-child-abuse-and-neglect.

Rahner, Karl. *Spirit in the World.* New York: Herder and Herder, 1968.

———. *Foundations of Christian Faith.* New York: Crossroad, 1978.

———. *Foundations of Christian Faith: An Introduction to the Idea of Christianity.* Concord: Paul & Company, 1982.

———. *Hearer of the Word: Layng the Foundation for a Philosophy of Religion.* London: Bloomsbury, 1994.

Randour, M. L., and J. Bondanza. "The Concept of God in the Psychological Formation of Females." *Psychoanalytic Psychology* (1987) 301–13.

Ratcliff, D. "Qualitative Data Analysis and the Transforming Moment." *Transformation: An International Journal of Holistic Mission Studies* 25 (2008) 116–33.

Rediger, G. L. "From Sickness to Well-Being." *Clergy Journal* 77 (2001) 14.

———. "Ministries of Health and Healing." *Clergy Journal* 78 (2002) 14.

Rizzuto, A. M. *The Birth of the Living God.* Chicago: University of Chicago Press, 1979.

Robinson, Tracy L. "Making the Hurt Go Away: Psychological and Spiritual Healing for African American Women Survivors of Childhood Incest." *Journal of Multicultural Counseling & Development* 28 (2000) 160–76.

Roche, D. N., M. G. Runtz, and M. A. Hunter. "Adult Attachment." *Journal of Interpersonal Violence* 14 (1999) 184–207.

Rogers, Carl. *Counseling and Psychotherapy.* Boston: Houghton Mifflin, 1942.

———. *Client-Centered Therapy: It's Current Practice, Implications and Theory.* London: Constable, 1951.

———. *A Way of Being.* Boston: Houghton Mifflin, 1980.

Rogers, C. R. "The Necessary and Sufficient Conditions of Therapeutic Personality Change." *Journal of Consulting Psychology* 21 (1957) 95–103.

Rosner, B. S., & McLean, L. M. "Theology and Human Flourishing: The Benefits of Being 'Known by God.'" In *Beyond Well-Being: Spirituality and Human Flourishing,* edited by M. Miner, M. Dowson, and S. Devenish, 65–83. Charlotte, NC: Information Age Publishing, 2012.

Rosner, B. S. "Known by God: C. S. Lewis and Dietrich Bonhoeffer." *Evangelical Quarterly* 77 (2005) 343–52.

Bibliography

Ryan, G. "Sexually Abusive Youth: Defining the Population." In *Juvenile Sexual Offending: Causes, Consequences, and Correction*, edited by G. Ryan and S. Lane, 3–9. San Francisco: Jossey-Bass, 1997.

Salter, A. C. "The Epidemiology of Child Sexual Abuse." In *The Sexual Abuse of Children: Vol. 1. Theory and Research*, edited by W. O'Donahue and J. H. Geer, 108–38. Hillsdale, NJ: Erlbaum & Associates, 1992.

Sarot, M. "Trinity and Church: Trinitarian Perspectives on the Identity of the Christian Community." *International Journal of Systematic Theology* 12 (2010) 33–45.

Sarwer, D. B., and J. A. Durlak. "Childhood Sexual Abuse as a Predictor of Adult Female Sexual Dysfunction: A Study of Couples Seeking Sex Therapy." *Child Abuse & Neglect* 20 (1996) 963–72.

Saunders, Daniel G. "Posttraumatic Stress Symptom Profiles of Battered Women: A Comparison of Survivors in Two Settings." *Violence and Victims* 9 (1994) 31–44.

Schleiermacher, Fredrich. *Christian Faith*. Edinburgh: T. & T. Clark, 1928.

Schmiechen, P. *Saving Power: Theories of Atonement and Forms of the Church*. Grand Rapids: Eerdmans, 2005.

Schmutzer, A. "A Theology of Sexual Abuse: A Reflection on Creation and Devastation." *Journal of the Evangelical Theological Society* 51 (2008) 785.

Shengold, L. *Soul Murder: The Effects of Childhood Abuse and Depression*. New Haven, CT: Yale University Press, 1989.

Shults, F. L., and A. Hollingsworth. *The Holy Spirit*. Grand Rapids: Eerdmans, 2008.

Siegel, Bernie S. *Love, Miracles and Medicine*. New York: Harper & Row, 1986.

Sinnott, J. D. "Introduction: Special Issue on Spirituality and Adult Development, Part I." *Journal of Adult Development* 8 (2001) 199–200.

Skinner, B. F. "Teaching Machines." *Science* 42 (1958) 969–77.

Smith, J. E. *Experience of God*. New York: Oxford University Press, 1968.

Sokolowski, R. *Introduction to Phenomenology*. New York: Cambridge University Press, 2007.

Spero, M. H. *Religious Objects as Psychological Structures: A Critical Integration of Object Relations Theory, Psychotherapy, and Judaism*. Chicago: University of Chicago Press, 1992.

Stoltenborgh et al., "A Global Perspective on Child Sexual Abuse: Meta-analysis of Prevalence around the World." *Child Maltreat* 16 (2011) 79–101.

Suchocki, M. "Theological Foundations for Ethnic and Gender Diversity in Faculties, or Excellence and the Motley Crew." *Theological Education* 26 (1990) 35–50.

Summit, R. C. "The Child Sexual Abuse Accommodation Syndrome." *Child Abuse and Neglect* 7 (1983) 177–93.

Tavard, G. H. "The Mystery of the Holy Spirit." *The Downside Review* 68 (1950) 255–70.

Taylor, H. *Sent to Heal: A Handbook on Christian Healing*. Ringwood, Australia: Order of St. Luke the Physician, 1993.

Taylor, J. V. *A Matter of Life and Death*. London: SCM, 1986.

———. *The Go-between God: The Holy Spirit and the Christian Mission*. London: SCM, 2004.

Terr, L. C. "Childhood Traumas: An Outline and Overview." *American Journal of Psychiatry* 148 (1991) 10–20.

Terry L. G., V. Basque, M. Damasceno-Scott, and G. Vardy, "Spirituality and the Current Adjustment of Adult Survivors of Childhood Sexual Abuse." *Journal for the Scientific Study of Religion* 46 (2007) 101–17.

Bibliography

Theron, J. P. J. "Towards a Practical Theological Theory for the Healing Ministry in Pentecostal Churches." *Journal of Pentecostal Theology* 7 (1999) 49–65.

Thomas, J. C. "Healing in the Atonement: A Johannine Perspective." *Journal of Pentecostal Theology* 14 (2005) 23–39.

Thompson, S. B. "Qualitative Research: Validity." *Journal of Administration and Governance* 6 (1991) 78–92.

Thorne, Brian. *Person-Centred Counselling: Therapeutic and Spiritual Dimensions.* London: Whurr Publishers, 1991.

Tillich, Paul. *Love, Power and Justice.* New York: Oxford University Press, 1960.

———. *Systematic Theology*, vol.2. Chicago: University of Chicago Press, 1957.

Tomison, A. M. "Update on Childhood Sexual Abuse." https://aifs.gov.au/cfca/publications/update-child-sexual-abuse.

Toynbee, B. *Towards the Holy Spirit.* London: SCM, 1973.

Ugeux, B. "The New Quest for Healing: When Therapy and Spirituality Intermingle." *International Review of Mission* 96 (2007) 22–40.

Valentine, LaNae, and Leslie L. Feinauer. "Resilience Factors Associated with Female Survivors of Childhood Sexual Abuse." *The American Journal of Family Therapy* 21 (1993) 216.

Van der Kolk, B. A., A. C. McFarlane, and L. Weisneth. *Traumatic Stress: The Effects of Overwhelming Experience on Mind, Body, and Society.* New York: Guilford, 1996.

Van der Watt, J. G. *Salvation in the New Testament: Perspectives in Soteriology.* Leiden: Brill, 2005.

Van Manen, M. *Researched Lived Experience: Human Science for an Action Sensitive Pedagogy.* Canada: Althouse, 1997.

Vanier, J. *Community and Growth.* London: St. Paul Publications, 1989.

Vining, John K. *Spirit-Centered Counseling.* New York: Cummings & Hathaway, 1995.

Volf, M. *The End of Memory: Remembering Rightly in a Violent World.* Grand Rapids: Eerdmans, 2006.

Warrington. K. "Acts and the Healing Narratives: Why?" *Journal of Pentecostal Theology* 14 (2006) 189–217.

———. "James 5:14–18: Healing Then and Now." *International Review of Mission* 93 (2004) 346–67.

Welker, M. *God the Spirit.* Minneapolis: Fortress, 1994.

———. *The Work of the Spirit: Pneumatology and Pentecostalism.* Grand Rapids: Eerdmans, 2006.

Williams, T. "God Who Sows the Seed and Gives the Growth: Anselm's Theology of the Holy Spirit." *Anglican Theological Review* 89 (2007) 611–27.

Wimber, J. *Power Evangelism: Signs and Wonders Today.* London: Hodder & Stoughton, 1986.

———. *The Dynamics of Spiritual Growth.* London: Hodder & Stoughton, 1991.

Winn, C. "Holy Spirit and the Christian Life." *Interpretation* 33 (1979) 47–57.

Winnicott, D. W. *The Maturation Processes and the Facilitating Environment.* London: Hogarth, 1965.

———. *Therapeutic Consultations in Child Psychiatry.* London: Hogarth, 1971.

Wise, C. W. *Pastoral Psychotherapy.* London: Jason Aronson, 1983.

Wright, J. "Profiles of Divine Healing: Third Wave Theology Compared with Classical Pentecostal Theology." *Asian Journal of Pentecostal Studies* 5 (2002) 271.

Wright, N. T. *The Resurrection of the Son of God.* Minneapolis: Fortress, 2003.

Bibliography

Zizioulas, J. D. *Being as Communion: Studies in Personhood and the Church.* New York: St. Vladimir's Seminary, 2002.

www.ingramcontent.com/pod-product-compliance
Lightning Source LLC
Chambersburg PA
CBHW062046220426
43662CB00010B/1667